WATERFALL WALKS
and DRIVES
in the
GREAT SMOKY MOUNTAINS
and the
WESTERN CAROLINAS

"To gaze on the sublimely grand spectacle, forms the grandest sight I ever beheld. Irregular and somewhat projecting rocks below, receive the water in its passage down, and breaks it into a perfect white foam which assumes a thousand forms in a moment. Sometimes flying up in jets of sparkling foam to the height of 15 or 20' and are scarcely formed before large, rolling bodies of the same deep and foaming water is thrown over and conceals them.... I wished that I might be enabled to give to the enlightened world some just idea of this truly magnificent and sublimely grand object, which has from the commencement of time been concealed from the view of civilized man."

Meriwether Lewis, on seeing the Great Falls of the Missouri, 1805.

I dedicate this book to Robert J. Ringer, whose books have taught me what freedom really is, and to the founding fathers of this country, and to those who hold their principles dear.

ACKNOWLEDGEMENTS

Many thanks to the Crocketts, owners of the Cooper Creek Trout Farm, for allowing us parking privileges and access to Little Creek Falls. Thanks to Mr. Richard Smith, for allowing public access to Connestee Falls. I am grateful to Ms. Marie Drew and Ms. Jo Sperry, of the Tryon Garden Club, for keeping Pearson's Falls in its natural state and allowing public access. I am very appreciative to the following good folks, for without their help this book would not have been possible: Mr. Carlton McNeill, for pointing me towards the highlights of the glorious Panthertown Valley; Mr. Joe Anderson, park superintendent at Caesar's Head State Park, for his invaluable information; my brother, Eric, for camping with me and helping me attain the book's most remote falls; to my parents, Jean and Henry, for their proofreading services; to my wife, Dee, for all of her help and support; last, but certainly not least, the many rangers and strangers for their help with this book.

Published by
H.F. Publishing, Inc.
4552 E. Elmhurst Dr.
Suite A
Douglasville, GA. 30135
USA

ISBN 0-9636070-3-0

Photos
Front cover: Little Creek Falls, GSMNP, NC. Back cover: Crabtree Falls, Blue Ridge Parkway, NC.

Printed in USA

INTRODUCTION

When people from this region think of waterfalls, usually Looking Glass or Whitewater Falls come to mind. These locations are very popular because of their great beauty and easy access. The intent of this book is to lead the reader to the lesser-known waterfalls in addition to these popular locations. I appreciate the "lesser knowns" for the solitude they provide. Many of them possess beauty that rivals or even exceeds that of the popular spots. Most are easily reached, requiring only a little more driving or footwork. By using a little common sense, they can be safely seen.

I enjoy researching the lesser knowns, then ferreting them out. Taking a topo map and finding my way through strange woods is a real challenge to the skills I acquired as a land surveyor. Surveying is a profession that I've been out of for many years, but still have in my blood. I love landscape photography and hiking, as well, so everything just fell in place, with the end result being these books.

Waterfalls are the "Gemstones of the East." Each one is faceted differently. Some have beauty that is big and bold, others have delicate and subtle characteristics. Common natural occurrences: rock, wood, and water attain their highest form when they come together as a waterfall. People who can't agree on anything else, seem to always agree on the beauty of a waterfall.

Although I know that I'm not the first person to see them, there are some locations that are so pristine that I feel like I am. I have visited at least 350 waterfalls. In doing so, I've obtained directions from handouts, area residents, and rangers. All too often the handouts had vague directions and just ended up getting me lost. I have been on dozens of "dry runs." I have experienced the frustration of traveling several miles down a road, only to find that I could go no further because of unknown road conditions, etc., while still facing miles of driving to a trailhead. I have also experienced the disappointment of being deep into a hike and finding that I could go no further, on account of high water or some other unknown obstacle. If I had only known the possible conditions beforehand, I might have altered my plans (waiting a few days for waters to recede after a rain, for instance). I wrote these books to provide accurate information so that you can make the most of your time.

You won't need a 4-wheel-drive vehicle or special hiking gear to visit the lesser knowns. On most of my visits I drove my light-duty pickup. (I did drive my jeep to visit the Panthertown Valley after a snow storm, however.) As far as hiking gear goes, you will need *at least* a pair of light hiking boots (see pg. IX for hiking essentials).

When negative is positive

Hiking is good therapy for the pressures of modern life. On top of that, studies have found that waterfalls soothe the savage beast. (They emit negative ions which counteract our stressful, positive ions.) The biggest challenge you'll probably face along the trail is, how to cross a creek without getting your feet wet. I know this isn't as adventuresome as searching for undiscovered Mayan temples, but if you take a closer look around you'll find new interests in things you never imagined. The woods are full of curiosities, such as birds, wildflowers, lichens, mushrooms, and unusual rock formations. I once considered these subjects commonplace and passé—I now find them intriguing. The more you hike, the more you'll become engrossed in things natural, both large and small.

I'm going to ask, up front, that you please haul out the trash that you haul in, plus whatever you find along the way. Harming natural features in any way is akin to defacing the Lincoln Memorial or other national treasures—an offense worthy of zero tolerance and strict penalties.

I'm amazed at the places that I find beer cans. I once found a can standing upright in the deep recess of a rock shelf. Someone had to get on their stomach, on wet rock, and extend their arm just as far as they could to place the can there. This is how some guys prove their manhood, I guess? I'll bet he really impressed his girl with that feat.

The National Forests, Parks, etc., belong to us—the taxpayers, not any individual. Therefore, no individual has the right to alter or destroy them. To minimize impact on these sensitive areas, please limit hiking party size to four persons.

Please leave pets at home. Dogs annoy other visitors and scare wildlife. I once came face to face with a wolf, or what I thought was a wolf. Knowing that wolves were extinct in the Southeast* I still took no chance and shed my pack for a hasty retreat. I then heard the wolf's owners coming up the trail. My wolf, turned out to be their Malamute.

Pets are not allowed on trails in the Smokies, at all. While hiking back from the Ramsay Cascades, however, I ran across a fellow who was getting a kick out of watching his dog running chipmunks.

Footbridges have a bad habit of disappearing during flash floods. At Whitewater Falls, a massive, hemlock log, complete with handrails, once spanned the river. In the early '90's it vanished along with the cables that held it in place. Although it has been replaced with a steel structure, don't be surprised if this dry route, and the others described in this book, have become driftwood or scrap iron.

*Wolves have recently been reintroduced into the Smokies.

When To Go

Go when they flow! Many of these spectacular falls will be disappointing in the dry months of summer and fall. I therefore recommend winter and spring visits. I find our mild Southern winters to be the best time of year to take a hike. Yes, the days are short, and yes, there are no flowers blooming, and yes, the trees are devoid of greenery. But winter is the season of heavy rains, bright white water, blue, haze-free sunny skies, no snakes, no bugs, no sweat, and no crowds. Lodging is cheap and plentiful then, too!

Trail "Happenings and Mishappenings"

Don't become a victim of, "walking dropsy syndrome." This is where you become so enamored while looking through the camera's viewfinder, that while jockeying for a better angle, you walk off a cliff.

Watch for poisonous snakes, or as my surveying buddy "Oink" Pozzi dubbed them, "no shoulders," for their lack of arms and legs. It seems that once you've seen a snake every root and downed tree limb looks like another one.

While photographing Schoolhouse Falls, in 8″ of snow, a couple of friendly dogs came upon me. Oblivious to my equipment, they licked and wagged and flailed all around me. I got to thinking, "for this type of weather they're sure a long way from home." Then I thought, "there might be someone behind these dogs." Sure enough, there was. Up trudged this older gentleman. He then proceeded to tell me everything he knew about the Panthertown Valley. His name, Carlton McNeill, probably *the* most knowledgeable person on the subject of this beautiful valley, and one very nice man.

While dodging the rain, in the Linville area, I stopped at a country store to enquire about a local waterfall. When I introduced myself to the proprietor, I was greeted with a, "Hi cuz!... I'm a Morrison too!" Turns out, we are distantly related. To commemorate this mini family reunion, I was offered a shot of moonshine and an expensive cigar. I passed on both. Being of Scotch descent, I thought he was going to don his kilt and break out the bagpipes.

Although *serious* and not funny *at all* at the time they occurred, here are some of the events I can now look back on and laugh about.

While hiking the Chattooga River Trail during 15° weather, I encountered a bedrock outcrop that I had tread upon many times before, in warm weather, with no problem. Being the wet season, and cold to boot, made this 200′ stretch of trail especially tricky. Water seeping onto the bedrock had frozen into a heavy glaze covering its entire length. The adjacent woods are so thick, and the mountainsides so steep, that I actually considered heading back to Burrell's Ford instead of exiting at Nicholson Ford (where my wife would be waiting). Instead, I hung on to anything I could grab, while I negotiated this mess on all fours, praying that I wouldn't slide into the river.

Before crossing the West Fork of the French Broad River, to check out a possible waterfall, I stood on the river bank and studied the situation. The river was 15′ wide, swift, and flowing over bedrock, but less than a foot deep. I had my cameras on my back and felt that my tripod, with legs extended, would be handy to probe the river's depths and for steadying myself while crossing. The first steps were easily made—just easy enough to entice me further into the river. Soon, I found myself in the middle of the river standing on bedrock that was slicker than ice. With rushing water about to knock me off my feet, I prayed..."Lord, I'll be good, if you'll just get me out of this one."

Before hiking the Slickrock Creek Trail, I inquired about the number of stream crossings we would encounter. I was told by some "knowledgeable" campers that there was only one ford between Wildcat and Lower Falls. To save weight we didn't take flip flops for stream crossing purposes. It turned out that there were 8 crossings between the falls, for a grand total of 12, from Big Fat Gap to Tapoco. Making these crossings barefooted, the soles of our feet were stone bruised almost to the bone. It seemed that every time we put our boots on, we were taking them right back off to recross the creek. But we persevered and completed this difficult hike. I'll never forget this adventure.

I'm sure you'll come away with waterfall memories as grand as mine. I wish you good fortune and hours of hiking enjoyment. May your feet stay forever dry.

Mark

The Happy Hiker

WORDS OF CAUTION

Crime

All too often I see evidence of cars having been broken into. Don't carry so much equipment that you become a prisoner of your possessions and are thus unable to enjoy yourself. Leave your valuables at home.

To hinder car thieves, use one of the popular steering wheel disablers and take the coil wire from your distributor. Use locking lug nuts to secure your wheels. Leave these opportunists the dust and ashes they deserve. Report suspicious activity.

Snake bites

Pit Vipers: Venom causes necrosis and pain. Treat with light constricting band and Sawyer Extractor. No cut and suck. Treat the wound, calm the victim, immobilize the extremity and evacuate for antivenin.

Coral Snake: Same treatment as above.

LIKE ANY OUTDOOR ACTIVITY, "WATERFALL WALKING" ISN'T WITHOUT ITS HAZARDS. THERE HAVE BEEN SEVERAL DEATHS AND INJURIES OF THOSE TRYING TO GET A CLOSER LOOK. NEVER JEOPARDIZE YOUR SAFETY BY GETTING INTO SOMETHING YOU CAN'T GET OUT OF. SAFETY MUST BE FIRST AND FOREMOST.

Rock climbing, spelunking, whitewater rafting and the like, have their own rules to minimize the risk of injury. "Waterfall Walking" has its common sense rules, too.

PLEASE REMEMBER THESE *DON'TS*:

1. DON'T VENTURE NEAR THE CLIFF EDGE FROM WHICH THEY FALL. THERE IS NO SCENERY OVER THE EDGE, SO WHY TAKE A CHANCE?

2. DON'T GET IN THE WATER UPSTREAM FROM THE FALLS. SIX INCHES OF WATER, IF MOVING FAST ENOUGH, CAN KNOCK YOU OFF YOUR FEET AND TAKE YOU OVER THE EDGE. BE MINDFUL THAT WATER MOVING ONLY 4 MILES AN HOUR EXERTS 66 POUNDS OF PRESSURE PER SQUARE FOOT. DEEP WATERS MAY *LOOK* STILL...ACTUALLY, WITH NOTHING TO IMPEDE ITS FLOW, DEEP WATER RUNS FAST.

WHEN FORDING A CREEK IN YOUR CAR, REMEMBER THAT TWO FEET OF WATER CAN SET IT AFLOAT.

3. DON'T BE FOOLED BY THE APPEARANCE OF SOLID GROUND. MOST OF THESE WATERFALL AREAS STAY PERPETUALLY WET FROM MIST AND HAVE A THIN LAYER OF LEAVES OR TOPSOIL HIDING *ALWAYS* SLICK ROCK, AND POSSIBLY ICE.

4. DON'T CLIMB THEM.

5. AS PREVIOUSLY MENTIONED, DON'T LEAVE VALUABLES IN YOUR CAR.

6. DON'T BLOCK GATES.

7. DON'T DRINK OR DRUG. VISIT THEM FOR THE NATURAL HIGH THEY INDUCE.

Please Do:

1. Take your camera along.

2. Bring along books on wildflowers, birds, and trees because I assure you that you'll be scratching your head, pondering the strange and beautiful sights, seen as you trek through the woods enroute to these waterfalls.

3. Haul out the litter that the inconsiderate have hauled in, leaving these sites naturally unaltered.

DISCLAIMER

The author and the publisher disclaim any liability or loss incurred as a consequence, directly or indirectly, of the use and application of any information contained in this book.

*　　*　　*　　*　　*

All trail distances in this book have been measured with a Rolatape measuring wheel.

All of the waterfalls contained in this book, *except* Connestee, Little Creek, Mingo, and Pearson's Falls, NC, are located on, and accessible via public lands. I have obtained permission to publish their locations and the landowners have been gracious enough to let us pass. Please respect the property of others, so that we may be invited back.

Periodically, Forest Service roads are closed on account of logging activity, or to protect the road from rutting during inclement weather. Check with the Forest Service before your visit.

HIKING ESSENTIALS

- Drinking water
- Waterproof matches
- Good, light, hiking boots, flip-flops to wear wading streams.
- A watch
- Flashlight
- High-energy foods
- Pocket knife
- Compass
- Benedryl, or similar medicines for reactions to stings.
- Moleskin for blisters.

Allow 30 minutes travel time for every level mile and 1 hour for every 1000' gain in elevation.

Never step into water unless you can see what you're getting into. As you cross, use a hiking stick or tripod to probe a safe route. Use this stick on your downstream side for steadiness. Probe for a sound steadying point before placing your weight on the stick, as you may lose your balance. Wear loose-legged pants to facilitate rolling them up above the knee. Unbuckle your backpack's waistbelt just in case you need to jettison your load. If you should fall in, point your feet downstream and protect your head with your hands and arms atop your head.

CONTENTS

Great Smoky Mountains National Park

Nantahala National Forest

Pisgah National Forest

Blue Ridge Parkway, Mile 364.6 - 268

Sumter National Forest

HOW TO USE THIS BOOK

This text is keyed to its maps and begins in the Great Smoky Mountains National Park of east Tennessee/western North Carolina and progresses easterly into North Carolina's Nantahala and Pisgah National Forests. After a trek up the Blue Ridge Parkway, the book takes in the stunning, western portion of South Carolina.

This book will lead you from a prominent landmark or intersection to individual waterfalls. Where there are several waterfalls in close proximity, they are listed in the order in which they are encountered from that landmark or intersection (see Holly Springs - Longcreek Area pg. 128).

Note in this example that #3, Brasstown Road, is 11.9 miles from the intersection of US Hwys. 76 West and 123 South in Westminster, SC, via Hwy. 76, and that #7, the Chattooga River Bridge (GA/SC state line) is 17.9 miles. To find the distance between them, simply subtract. The two points are 6 miles apart. In the same example, if you wanted to drive from #7, the Chattooga River Bridge, to #4, Damascus Church Road, your distance would be 17.9 minus 13.2 equaling 4.7 miles.

Listed along with each waterfall is:

(1) The worst road conditions encountered: Graveled, etc. (See the example below.)

(2) A beauty scale of 1 (worth seeing), through 10 (a knockout).

(3) The waterfall's height (if known).

(4) The USGS topographic map on which the waterfall is shown.

(5) The official trail number (if known).

(6) The one-way hiking distance, and/or time required to reach them (unless noted in the text).

(7) Water crossings (if any) and the effort needed to reach the falls (easy, through difficult). See definitions.

---

(1) Roads: Graveled   (2) A "10" (3) 30'
(4) USGS Quadrangle: Holly Springs, SC
(5) Trail #, (6) .8 of a mile, (7) water crossing, moderate

ABBREVIATIONS:

BT= The Bartram Trail
FT= The Foothills Trail
CRT= The Chattooga River Trail
FS= Forest Service, designating a Forest Service road.

DEFINITIONS:

Carsonite stake: A trade name for a fiberglass-type stake used to mark roads and trails.

Path: An unmaintained treadway.

Trail: A maintained treadway.

Very Easy: A smooth treadway over level ground.

Easy: Uneven ground, but fairly level.

Moderate: Some steep grades, some level sections of trail.

Difficult: Steep grades, uneven terrain and long, steady climbs.

Graveled: A road that most automobiles without airdams could negotiate, except where noted.

High Clearance: A road that most pickup trucks could negotiate.

USGS Quadrangle: A US Geological Survey topo map.

KEY TO MAP SYMBOLS:

★ = A landmark from which the text begins.

A,1,b, etc.: Italicized letters or numbers on Area Maps represent waterfall locations or landmarks with mileage given in the text. Numbers subdivide capital letters; lower case letters subdivide numbers, etc.

Contour intervals on hiking maps are 40' unless otherwise noted.

▬▬▬▬▬▬	Paved Roads
════════	Graveled or Dirt Roads
▬ ▬ ▬ ▬ ● ● ● ● ●	Trails and Pathways
▬▬▬ ● ● ● ▬▬▬	Rivers and Creeks
P	Parking
●━━●	Gate

(40) =Interstate Hwy. (64) =US Hwy. (28) =Primary State Hwys.

(159) =Secondary Roads **340** =Forest Service Roads

Where the word "gate" is used, in the field you may find boulders or earthen mounds, instead.

In the field, double blazes represent sudden or unexpected changes in trail direction. They are also used to call attention to trail junctions. Also, where there is no tree to blaze, rocks may be stacked on top of one another in cairn fashion. Where bedrock is exposed, look for blazes painted directly on the rock.

PHOTOGRAPHING WATERFALLS

Most people don't seem to associate photography with work. My guess is that they associate "taking pictures" with being on vacation (having fun). "How could that be work?" they must ask themselves. I think you'll find serious photography very hard work. The knowledge of how to use cameras, lenses, and films takes a great deal of time and expense to acquire. Lugging equipment into remote locales and up and down mountainsides is often arduous. Standing in the midst of breathtaking scenery and capturing it on film, with the results *you* want, is ample reward for these hardships.

Good images take careful planning. In the case of waterfalls, being there at the right time is of the utmost importance. During dry periods, usually summer and fall, or under drought conditions, many locations have greatly reduced water volumes that make them less photogenic. Also, with this high-contrast subject, you must utilize the best natural lighting conditions.

Successful photography begins with a good camera system. There are several brands and camera models in the 35mm format that fit the bill. I prefer a manual camera, such as the Nikon FM2, for its simplicity and wide array of available accessories.

Many of these waterfalls have to be photographed closely because of view-blocking rocks, trees, and vegetation. The 46° field of view of a normal lens (a 50mm lens) in most cases is not wide enough to encompass an entire waterfall, close-up. Nikon makes a 24-50mm wide-angle zoom lens which is ideal for most waterfall photography, having an 84 to 46° range of coverage. This lens also has macro capabilities making it useful in photographing wildflowers, as well. (Watch carefully for lens flare with this lens. This condition may not be readily apparent through the viewfinder, but during long exposures it will be on film.)

Use a tripod and shutter-release cable at all shutter speeds. This eliminates the possibility of camera shake and ensures the sharpest images. These items also allow you to make long exposures for smooth-flowing, velvet-like water.

Depth of field: Generally, depth of field lies 1/3 in front of, and 2/3 behind the object of focus. For example: If the object of focus is 50' away, the nearest object in sharp focus would be located at 33', while the farthest object would be at 83'. All objects within that range will be in sharp focus. Focusing in this way (on the subject only) wastes alot of depth of field.

To remedy this, stop the lens down and focus *hyperfocally*. Apertures of $f/8$ to $f/22$ yield greater depth of field and thus sharper images. Learn how to set the depth of field for any given aperture. It's very simple to do and you can obtain images that are sharp from front to back by setting your lens properly. For example, with the aperture on my 50mm lens set at $f/22$, if I set the far depth-of-field distance (infinity on the focusing ring, in this example) in line with f/22 on the far depth-of-field scale, the near depth-of-field distance automatically lines up with f/22 on the *near* depth-of-field scale, and reads 6 1/2'. (This yields a "hyperfocal distance" [where the object of focus lies] of 12 1/2'.) This means that all objects between 6 1/2' and infinity will be in sharp focus. Even though the scene appears out of focus in the viewfinder, it will be rendered *on film* with front-to-back sharpness. Compose the shot with this in mind, keeping objects that are too close (since they would not be sharp) out of the frame. Better cameras, like the FM2, have a depth-of-field preview button to let you see the stopped-down results in advance.

Metering: Try to shoot in evenly-lighted conditions. High-contrast lighting produces poor photos. Our eyes have an eleven-stop light range. Films don't have the ability to record this wide tonal range. In order to come away with the best images, we need to learn to see as the film sees.

Print films can "see" a range of light, or have a *latitude* of 7 stops, with 5 stops being optimum. Slide films have a 5 stop latitude, with 3 being optimum. Meter your subject with this in mind. If there is an area in the viewfinder that is either too bright, or too dark, recompose the shot to eliminate the unwanted area, or wait for even lighting. Remember, with most cameras, the viewfinder only covers around 93% of a scene, or you may inadvertently include part of the unwanted area.

When metering, leave the waterfall out of the equation. Meter for mid-toned rock or light-green foliage in the same light as the waterfall. If you meter for the much brighter waterfall itself, you'll end up with gray water and silhouettes of the surroundings. For more accurate exposures, use an 18% gray card in the same light as the subject. You may have a camera bag that is close enough to 18% gray to use in lieu of a gray card.

When using slow films in very low-light conditions, you can obtain a useable shutter speed by switching the camera's film speed dial to a faster film speed setting. If, for instance, you are using 50 speed film, set the aperture on your lens to obtain the depth of field you desire, then set the film speed dial to, let's say, 200 (used here for ease of calculation, you can use 100, 400, 1000, or whatever film speed setting it takes to get a reading). Take a meter reading of a mid-toned area in the scene. Now, multiply that reading by 4, since 50 (the actual film speed) divided into 200 (the metered speed) = 4. If you had a shutter speed reading of say, 1 second, expose the film for 4 seconds. If your camera's shutter speed dial doesn't allow for exposures of over 1 second, set the dial to the "bulb" setting and time the shot yourself, by counting, one thousand one, one thousand two, etc. (Afterwards, be sure to reset the film speed dial back to your correct film speed setting to avoid later metering errors.)

Films are engineered to react to light within certain parameters. When used outside these time frames, they react differently, i.e., colors may not be true, contrast may change, or the film may be underexposed. Call or write the film's manufacturer for a data sheet which gives details of the film's characteristics, including, "reciprocity failure." Reciprocity failure is the failure of film to record light accurately when used outside the limits for which it was designed. With Fujichrome Velvia and Provia films there is no correction needed for exposures of 4 seconds, or less. With Kodachrome 25 and 64 speed films, allow 1/2 and 1 stop more exposure, respectively, when exposing at 1 second or slower, or your shots will come out underexposed.

Exposure: To show the power of a large waterfall, stop the action with the use of a medium speed film, ISO 100 or 200, and a fast shutter speed, 1/125TH of a second or faster. Plan to shoot on a bright, sunny day so that the sharper, small apertures can be used. In general, large waterfalls look unnatural when long exposures are used. With lots of bright water, long exposures may "wash out" the film, rendering the waterfall portion of the image totally featureless.

Small, or low-volume waterfalls photograph best under shady or overcast conditions. This allows the use of small apertures, for sharpness, and long exposures to softly blur the water. Use films rated ISO 25 to 100 for their long exposure tolerances and fine grain. With low-volume waterfalls there is less chance of washing the film out.

When using slow shutter speeds it's hard to obtain good shots on windy days unless you can exclude windblown vegetation from the frame.

Bracket your shots. Expose at the metered reading, then expose at least 1 stop over, and 1 stop under, in 1/2 stop increments. This assures that you'll have at least one correct exposure.

Composition: Fill the frame with your subject. I have often made the mistake of trying to include too much in a photo, with the end result being a dinky waterfall lost among the other detail.

On sunny days, a rainbow may be found in the mist, in an arc that hangs 42° from the antisolar point. The antisolar point lies exactly 180° opposite the sun, and is marked by the shadow of the observer's head.

The "rule of thirds" works well in waterfall photography. This common composition technique catches, then leads the viewer's eye into a photo. Divide the viewfinder into thirds with two imaginary vertical lines and then two imaginary horizontal lines—like a tic-tac-toe board. When shooting either vertically or horizontally, place the subject *at* or *near* one of the four positions where these lines cross. Compose the shot with the waterfall flowing freely into and across the frame.

Avoid "Keystoning" if possible. This occurs when the camera is tilted up or down. (In the case of most waterfalls, since we will be at the base looking up, I'll use the following example.) Since the subject is closer to the film plane at the bottom and farther away at the top, a lens renders it much larger at the bottom and smaller at the top (like a pyramid, or inverted keystone) than it appears to our naked eyes. Wide-angle lenses exaggerate this distortion. To avoid this, try shooting the subject straight on (parallel to the film plane) if possible. Special lenses called, "perspective-control," or "PC" lenses correct this distortion to a degree, but they are expensive.

Films: I almost always shoot slide film for the sharpness and intense colors it is capable of recording. I'm partial to Fujichrome Velvia (50 speed) and Provia (100 speed) films for their fine grain, true colors, and ease of processing. Kodak has several fine films that are suited for waterfall photography, as well. Kodak EPR 64, E 100S, and E 100SW films have good latitude and are able to handle highlight and shadow detail better than the aforementioned Fuji films.

Many times these films are not fast enough for the conditions I'm shooting in. If I need the extra speed, to freeze action, or for increased depth of field, I push these films by 1 stop. This is done by changing the camera's film speed setting. For example, with 50 speed film set the meter to 100, with 100 speed film set it to 200. The film is thus underexposed by 1 stop in the camera. To compensate for this, it must be overexposed or "pushed" by 1 stop in the first developer, during processing. Mark the cassette, as such, and be sure to ask for push processing, which is slightly more expensive.

If you need to slow a film down, use a polarizing filter. A polarizing filter will reduce the light entering the lens by 2 stops, allowing for longer exposure times. Carefully turn the filter and observe its effect on the wet rock, foliage, and the blue sky (which will be rendered a deeper blue if the camera is pointed at right angles to the sun). This filter, through its glare reduction, saturates the film with color and thus enhances the image. If this filter is used improperly the rock's glistening sheen will look flat and unnatural. A neutral density filter will also reduce light transmission, but I find a polarizer far more handy.

Photographing in shade, during the early morning and late afternoon hours, slide films will record the surroundings with a steely-blue cast. This occurs because daylight-balanced films are designed to be used in the interim between 2 hours after sunrise and 2 hours before sunset, when warmer light is present. This blue cast can be corrected with a warming filter.

For black-and-white photography I like the sharpness of Kodak T-Max 100 speed negative film. This film can also be pushed 1 stop without having to overdevelop to compensate for its underexposure. This means that this film is actually a 100 and 200 speed film built into one, whose speed can be switched in mid-roll, if you need the additional speed for increased depth of field, or to freeze action. This mid-roll switch is not possible with slide or color negative films.

Black-and-white and color print films can bail you out in bad lighting situations. These films can record the shots that slide films can't. Negative film can be overexposed in the field, then manipulated in the darkroom, to print the detail you actually saw in the field.

Misc. conditions: In the cold of winter you may run into the unattractive curling of rhododendron leaves. This self corrects as daytime temperatures rise.

XVII

Great Smoky Mountains National Park

Established June 15th, 1934, and designated an International Biosphere Reserve in 1976, Great Smoky Mountains National Park is comprised of 520,408 acres (approximately 800 square miles) in western North Carolina and eastern Tennessee. Scattered within its confines are more than 100,000 acres of virgin forest—the most extensive stands in the East. More varieties of trees and vegetation reside in the park than on the entire European Continent. The park boasts more than 1500 species of flowering plants—more than are found at any North American national park. With more than 9,000,000 visitors annually, it is the most heavily visited of our National Parks.

Two hundred seventy miles of roads access over 800 miles of hiking trails. It seems that most visitors stick close to their cars and visit points of interest along the most heavily-traveled routes, US 441 and Little River Road. Even with the large crowds there are still quiet places to be found. The Cosby, Greenbrier, Tremont, and Twentymile areas are but a few of the park's less-visited locales.

Park elevations range from 874', at the mouth of Abrams Creek, to 6643' atop Clingmans Dome (the 3rd highest peak in the East). Plant zones range from temperate, found at lower elevations, to subalpine, at the highest. This wide zonal range is equivalent to a 1000 mile trip to the north.

Dress for the occasion

Remember, especially on extended or high-country hikes, that the weather can change suddenly and that temperatures drop approximately 3 degrees Fahrenheit for each 1000' gain in elevation. Temperatures in the high country can be from 10 to 15 degrees cooler than those in the lower elevations.

Other park facts:

- 125 tree species
- 50 varieties of ferns
- 350 species of mosses and liverworts
- 230 lichen species
- 2000+ species of mushrooms and fungi
- 200 types of birds have been observed of which 60 are permanent residents
- 58 varieties of fish
- 60 mammal species
- 80 types of reptiles and amphibians that include 23 snake varieties (2 poisonous, the timber rattler, and northern copperhead), and 27 types of salamanders.

Why the mountains are smoky

The Smokie's great forests transpire moisture into the atmosphere causing the distinct haze for which the park was named. Mature trees give off tons of water to the atmosphere. On a summer day a large tree may give off up to 900 gallons of water.

Mountain history

The Cherokee name for these mountains is "Shaconage," meaning "Place of Blue Smoke." The Smoky Mountains are rich in history—both natural and human. There are excellent publications that delve deeply into the region's fascinating history. A free publication, available from the Gatlinburg Chamber of Commerce, *Great Smoky Mountains National Park,* and an auto tour booklet, *Tremont Logging History,* available for a nominal fee, published by the Great Smoky Mountains Natural History Association, are very informative.

I find myself intrigued by the events of the last 200 years. This region was the heart of the Cherokee Nation. They, along with other southern tribes, were forcibly relocated to Western lands. Between 1838 and 1839 U.S. Troops rounded up all but a few of their people. Those who eluded capture took refuge in the rugged mountains of western North Carolina. The Trail of Tears, as it became known, is a dark moment in American history, when a people were dispossessed of their lands. Thousands were rounded up, many plucked from the fields as they worked, then herded into stockades to await their removal. The forced march took the captives to "Indian Territory" (Oklahoma). Enroute, some 4,000 Cherokee, one fourth of the tribe, died. In 1889 the eastern band of the Cherokee came out of their mountain hideouts and found refuge on the 56,000 acre "Qualla Boundary" near the town of Cherokee, North Carolina, where some 11,000 of their descendants reside today. The Qualla Boundary is *not* a reservation, but land bought and paid for by the Cherokee and held in trust by the Federal Government.

In the late 19th and early 20th centuries, timber interests, having depleted northern forests, bought into the southern mountains for their virgin timbers. Extensive logging was carried out in the Smokies between 1885 and 1939, leaving much of these mountains a wasteland. Over 20 lumber companies and dozens of sawmills worked these mountains. At the time of the park's establishment only one fourth of its land lay relatively undisturbed. Having made such an astounding recovery, it's hard to imagine these mountains so devastated.

Logging reached deep into the mountains via rail. Rail-mounted skidders, some with overhead cables (much like a ski lift), winched logs off the mountainsides from as far as a mile away. Another removal method was to drag logs with draft animals over pole roads to trackside points where they were loaded onto flatcars. Camp-like communities with churches, company stores and schools thrived—relocating as the work did. Women raised crops and tended to the household chores while the men worked six, ten hour days, either logging or in support trades.

Many of the trails we will hike are old logging railroad beds. In places, you will see remnants of the old days, rail, spikes, tie plates, bridges, cables, etc.

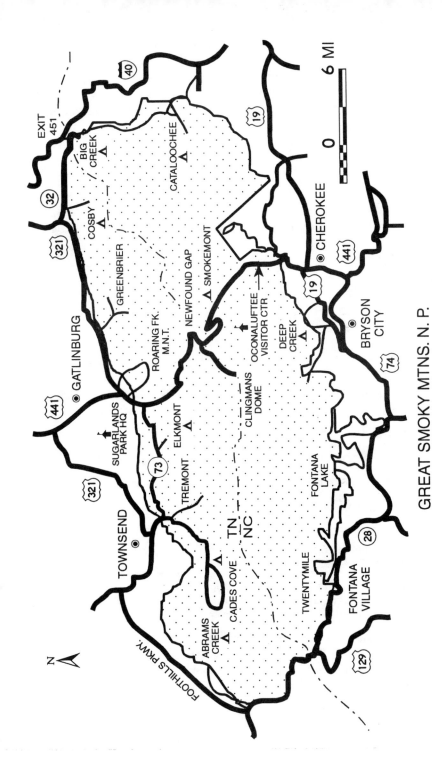

GREAT SMOKY MTNS. N. P.

Enroute to the Ramsay Cascades, you will pass through a beautiful virgin forest. I talked to a fellow who was busy measuring three of the giants. He proclaimed, "...this one's 19'(in circumference), that one's 16', the other one's 14'." They were the largest trees (poplar), of any variety, that I've ever seen. One day, perhaps 200 years from now, the hollows and mountainsides that were logged will have the grand giants once again.

"A-B" Cades Cove and Tremont Area

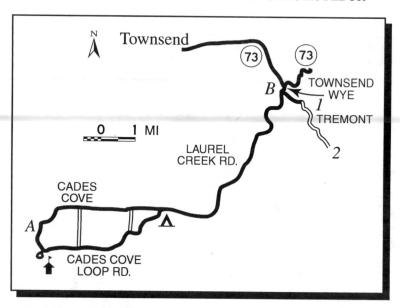

A. Abrams Falls

Roads: Graveled   A "10"
USGS Quadrangles: Cades Cove & Calderwood, TN, NC
Abrams Falls Trail, 2.55 miles, minor water crossings, moderate-difficult

A. Directions: From the Townsend Wye, take Laurel Creek Road to the Cades Cove Loop Road. Drive the loop to its apex and follow the signs to the Abrams Falls Trail parking area.

Enter the woods on the west end of the parking area. In 170' look for a sign that states, " Abrams Falls Trail, Abrams Falls 2.5 miles." At 220' cross Abrams Creek on a footbridge. Now on the creek's west side, at 305', the fall's trail splits left, while the Wet Bottom Trail, which accesses the Elijah Oliver Place, leads right (signs give directions and distances). The fall's trail soon bends right to head west, treading level under overhanging rhododendron. At around 600' the trail begins an undulating ascent alongside a river-sized

4

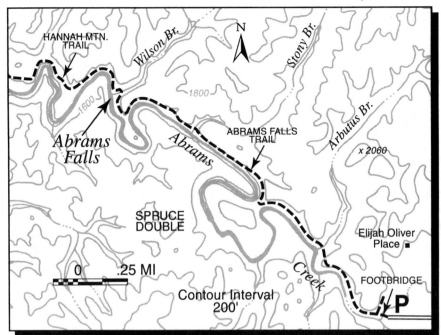

Abrams Creek. (The creek has doubled in size since the initial crossing, as the unseen Mill Creek joined from the left.) At .4 of a mile the rate of ascent steepens. At .55 of a mile top out in a small, open area. The trail makes a bend to the north here and momentarily loses sight of the creek. Now descending at a moderate rate, arrive back at creek level (.65 of a mile). Shortly thereafter, with a right and left bend, the trail crosses the rather large Arbutus Branch on the first footlog-type footbridge. Rejoining and treading level alongside the shoaling Abrams Creek, at .95 of a mile, cross a small seep that is culverted through a stone buildup. Soon thereafter, the trail turns uphill and away from the creek while treading a rocky stretch. At 1.1 miles the trail tops out at a large, sandstone outcrop. Running level for 165′, it then passes through a scenic, rock cut gap. The trail now turns sharply right and descends while heading northeasterly. Still descending, at 1.2 miles, the trail now trends more northerly with Abrams Creek out of sight 200-300′ to the left, and almost that high above it. With a right bend, at 1.4 miles, enter the hollow of a culverted branch. Completing the outline of its hollow, rejoin Abrams Creek (1.5 miles) and enter a long straightaway, at times passing through tunnels of rhododendron. At 1.8 miles cross the second footlog footbridge, this one spanning Stony Branch. At 2.05 miles the trail makes a noticeable ascent. Approximately 150′ above creek level (at 2.25 miles), the trail tops out, soon bends right, descends and narrows. At 2.4 miles pass Abrams Falls which is far below trail level and barely visible through the woods. Soon thereafter, tread upon an especially rocky and root-laced stretch while entering the cove of Wilson Branch. At 2.5 miles the trail turns sharply left to cross the sliding waters of Wilson Branch, on the third footlog. Following the north side of this creek downstream, in 260' (2.55 miles into the hike) arrive at a trail sign stating, "Abrams Falls." (The Hannah Mountain Trail continues to the right, following Abrams Creek downstream.) With a left turn, recross Wilson Branch on the fourth footlog and hike up Abrams Creek a rocky 150' to the base area.

Twenty feet high and 20' wide, Abrams Falls pours over a rock ledge into a deep plunge pool that extends 100' out from the base. Alder trees grow on the left side of its 100'-wide pool and thick rhododendron grows on the slopes to the right. Hemlock and hardwoods fill the background. A large, jagged, bedrock cliff compliments the left side.

Abrams Falls photographs best when lit by the afternoon sun, or on an overcast day. I've never seen this waterfall depicted as beautifully as it actually is.

Bleeding heart, flame azalea and galax are seen trailside.

Tremont Area

B. Directions: From the intersection of TN 73 and Laurel Creek Road (the Townsend Wye) drive west for just over .2 of a mile (crossing the Middle Prong bridge enroute) to Tremont Road. (A sign preceding the intersection states, "Great Smoky Mountains Institute.") Turn left and drive the following distances to the points of interest listed below. (Tremont Road is paved to the institute and graveled thereafter.)

1. The turnoff for the Great Smoky Mountains Institute at Tremont (access to Spruce Flats Falls): 2 miles.
2. The parking area and Middle Prong Trailhead (access to the Falls of Lynn Camp Prong and Indian Flats Falls): 5.15 miles.

1. Spruce Flats Falls

Roads: Paved   A "5" 25'
USGS Quadrangle: Wear Cove, TN
.95 of a mile, moderate-difficult, minor water crossings, steep drop-offs

Directions: Turn left onto the access road for the Great Smoky Mountains Institute at Tremont. Cross the Middle Prong of the Little River and in .05 of a mile look for trail parking on the right. (The Tremont Institute's headquarters are on the left at this location.) The paved road, which the route initially treads, is located at the southeast end of this parking area.

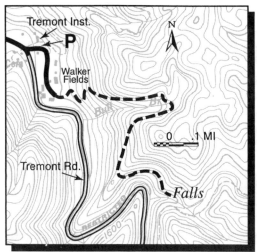

Initially heading south, via this paved road, pass the basketball court and ballfield (Walker Fields). At 900', after passing the staff housing, the trail enters the woods on in-ground steps at a sign stating, "Falls Trail." The trail immediately bends left and ascends via switchbacks while heading in a northeasterly direction. At the midpoint of the second switchback pass a water tank, which is on the right. At .3 of a mile a potentially confusing pathway leads straight ahead while the fall's trail turns right. With a left bend (.35 of a mile) round a point of land and head southeasterly up a steep cove. Admire the beautiful mountain views to the south from this area. Looming across the river to the southwest is Fodderstack Mountain. The trail is rocky, rooty, and narrow along this stretch and sports some steep drop-offs. At .45 of a mile, in a shallow hollow, cross a small, rocky, wet-weather branch. The treadway immediately traverses rubble-like rock then steepens while undulating over rock and roots. In a slightly deeper rocky cove (.55 of a mile) cross Bull Branch. (The trail seems to disappear amongst the rock, but continues straight ahead, ascending at a moderate to difficult rate.) After leveling briefly the trail turns uphill. At a saddle-like point of land turn left (northeast) amongst the laurel. High above a deep river bend, veiled, equidistant views of the river are presented. Undulating while descending, at times over rock and roots, at .8 of a mile you may notice several large boulders protruding out of the south face of the mountain. Descending more steeply from this point, at .9 of a mile the trail turns sharply left to enter the fall's cove. At .95 of a mile reach the fall's viewing area.

A 4 to 5' fall, in front of the viewer, precedes the larger one (seen upstream). Approximately 25' high and 20' wide, Spruce Flat's main flow is over the right side of the bedrock exposure. There is an upper prelude to them that is just barely seen in the distance. A small, 25 by 25' pool lies at their base.

2. Falls of Lynn Camp Prong and Indian Flats Falls

Roads: Graveled   A "9" & "7" respectively
USGS Quadrangle: Thunderhead Mtn., TN, NC
Middle Prong Trail, .65 and 3.9 miles respectively, minor water crossings, moderate (with rocky stretches)

Wildflowers abound on this trail. Fringed phacelia grows in multi-acre, woodland colonies. The handbook, *Wildflowers of the Smokies*, is correct in stating that they ..."are so densely packed it can look as if a light snow has recently fallen."

The parking area is located at the once bustling, logging community of Tremont. All manner of buildings were present here: a machine shop; and a combination church, school, and theatre. To the southeast, a 20+ room hotel once stood. Built for employees, it later served as a resort. As you cross Lynn Camp Prong on the old iron railroad bridge, you stand in the vicinity of where the post office/company store once stood.

Directions: At this location look for the old iron railroad bridge that now serves as a footbridge (approximately 100′ due south of the parking area). The hike begins at the north end of the bridge.

Northbound, in 140′ a side path leads right to access the Thunderhead Prong drainage. Stay left and at 335′ pass a trail sign which states, "Middle Prong Trail," with various destinations listed, as well.

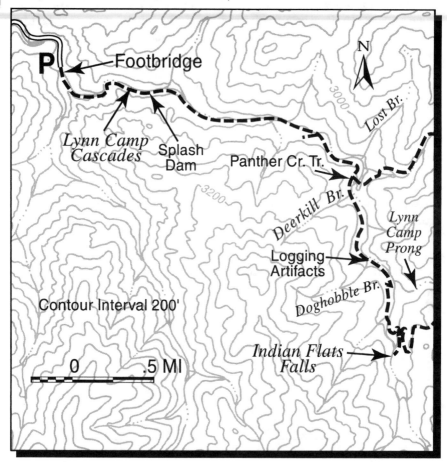

Initially, the Middle Prong Trail ascends at an easy to moderate rate alongside Lynn Camp Prong (a major tributary of the Middle Prong of the Little River). At .35 of a mile arrive at a log bench and viewing area of Lynn Camp Prong's cascades. Continuing upstream, the trail makes a hard left in conjunction with the mountainside and cascading stream. Sandstone outcrops with walls of 30 to 40′flank the trail's right side. Continuing its ascent, the trail soon levels alongside the top of this lengthy cascade (.45 of a mile). After a brief ascent, the trail once again levels at a log bench view of the Falls of Lynn Camp Prong (.65 of a mile). Pause here to enjoy the grandeur of this stairstepping waterfall.

Creekside, at .7 of a mile, look for the bolts, timbers, and stoneworks of a splash dam. These structures were used by early loggers to impound creeks and logs. When sufficient water had built up, the dam was breached. The ensuing surge floated the logs downstream. At 1.35 miles look for a triple cascade with a deep, foaming green hole at its base. Boulders on the far side of the stream are balanced atop lesser ones. In the vicinity of 1.75 miles several paths take off to the right, leading to the remains of an old car. Fringed phacelia covers acres of ground here. Exiting a south bend, at 2.35 miles arrive at the junction of the Panther Creek Trail. (Signs give directions and distances.)

The Middle Prong Trail now bends left in harmony with the river. At the bend's midpoint, a beautiful view of the tumbling river is presented, both up and downstream. At 2.45 miles cross Deerkill Branch on steppingstones. Soon thereafter, pass over a small creek flowing through a culvert. This creek has its beginnings in an upland bog whose trailside upper extremes are located at mile 2.7. Above the bog is a small meadow loaded with foamflower and trillium. At 2.95 miles look for an old brick fireplace 50′ to the trail's left. Further investigation yields a nearby concrete foundation with bolts cemented in place. Soon thereafter, pass a moss-covered, stacked rock wall to the trail's right. Just ahead, in an opening to the left, you may notice a switch point (a 15′ piece of rail) and other artifacts from the logging days.

Entering the drainage of Indian Flats Prong (3.2 miles) the trail makes a sharp right and switchbacks up the mountainside. From this point to the falls, the hike is rated moderate. At 3.45 miles cross a small branch flowing through an exposed culvert. In 110′ cross Double Trestle Branch on steppingstones. Soon bending left, the trail dips to cross Indian Flats Prong on a footbridge. (In spring, bluets beautifully carpet the stream's rock.) Now on the east side of the infant river, the trail makes an abrupt right and heads upstream. With a left turn, at 3.6 miles, the trail turns away from the creek then soon switchbacks up the mountainside. At the top of the *first* and beginning of the *second* switchback (3.8 miles) look for a slim, unmarked path entering the doghobble and rhododendron (on the right). Duck, bob, and weave your way upstream through this heavy growth for 475′ to the base of the upper tier.

Indian Flats Falls consists of 4 tiers. The upper tier is 8' high and enters the scene as a small, narrow stream which is split into two major flows. To the right, its plunge pool is dammed by thousands of rounded stones—what would be an island, during high water, dams the pool's left side. The stream's main flow exits the pool's right side, enroute to the 2nd, 3rd, and 4th tiers which have a combined run length of approximately 200'.

In spring, common trailside flowers, include: bluets, Fraser's sedge, foam-flower, jack-in-the-pulpit, violets, and showy orchis.

Sugarlands Area and Sugarlands West

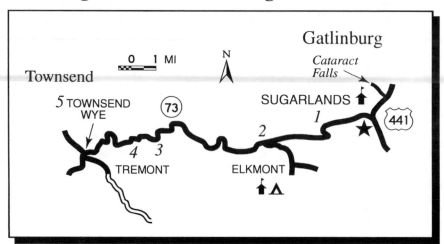

Sugarlands Area

Cataract Falls

Roads: Paved   A "4"
USGS Quadrangle: Gatlinburg, TN (No hiking map needed.)
Cove Mountain Trail, .1 of a mile, easy

Directions: From the intersection of US 441 and Little River Road (TN 73), at the Sugarlands Visitor and Information Center, drive north on 441 for just under .2 of a mile and turn left onto the park headquarters access road. Drive another .1 of a mile and turn left. Look for the parking area 200' ahead on the right. The route to the falls (via the Cove Mountain Trail) begins at the northwest corner of the stone bridge over Fighting Creek.

Hike the level but winding treadway downstream, passing through a rhododendron and hemlock forest. At 490' the trail bends sharply left.

Continue another 150' to the fall's viewing area.

Six to eight feet wide, with its flow split by the bedrock, this tumbling, 20', whitewater cascade shoals towards the viewer. The greater portion of the creek flows over the right side of the bluff. At times the left side may be dry. Moss covers the rock on its left side. Rhododendron and hemlock surround the exposure. Cataract Creek then flows north to join Fighting Creek. A mere trickle in all but the wettest months, with adequate water this is a very beautiful waterfall.

The Cove Mountain Trail continues to the right, crossing Cataract Creek. Cataract Falls photographs best under the diffused light of an overcast day.

Sugarlands West

Directions: From US 441, at the Sugarlands Visitor Center, drive west on Little River Road (TN 73) to the following points of interest:

1. Parking for Laurel Falls: 3.8 miles.
2. The turnoff for the Elkmont Campground (access to the Huskey Branch Cascades): 5 miles.
3. Parking for the Sinks: 11.8 miles.
4. The pullout for Meigs Falls: 12.9 miles.
5. The intersection of Laurel Creek Road and TN 73 (the Townsend Wye): 17.65 miles.

1. Laurel Falls

Roads: Paved   A "6"
USGS Quadrangle: Gatlinburg, TN
Laurel Falls self-guiding nature trail, 1.25 miles, easy-moderate

Note: Keep close tabs on children at the unprotected exposures. Because of heavy usage the Laurel Falls Trail is paved from parking lot to plunge pool. If you're wearing hard-soled hiking boots the pavement becomes very slick when wet.

This self-guiding nature trail is keyed to a brochure. The brochure is available (for a small fee) at the Sugarlands Visitor Center, or at the trailhead.

The Laurel Falls Trail enters the woods on the north side of the parking area and immediately turns west. At approximately 300' the trail begins its meandering, easy ascent of the south slopes of Cove Mountain. At just under .4 of a mile a rushing Pine Knot Branch makes its presence known on the left. While passing through a hardwood forest, at .5 of a mile, cross this rushing branch. Three fourths of a mile into the hike, at a notable point of land, the trail

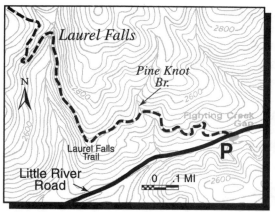

tops out and makes a bend to the north. At .85 of a mile look for a beautiful, window-like view to the west. This is a great spot to photograph at sunrise or sunset with the distant mountains filling the foreground. Along this stretch of trail are numerous sandstone outcrops. Laurel and rhododendron crowd the steep slopes.

As the trail turns northeast and begins to descend (1.1 miles), an unseen Laurel Branch, far below, audibly makes its presence known. One and two-tenths miles into the hike, carefully pass an unprotected exposure, on the left, with a 100'+ drop-off. On the final approach to the falls take note of the beautiful cliffs to the right. Approximately 50' high, they are covered colorfully in mosses, lichens, rock tripe, and ferns. After hiking 1.25 miles arrive at the concrete bridge and viewing area for Laurel Falls.

Laurel Falls spills from a 6'-wide flowway that occupies the right side of the bedrock exposure. Smooth bedrock, with slight depressions, flanks the left side. The first portion is 10' high and broken into several cascades. (If Laurel Branch is running high, some of its swift waters shoot out far enough to clear the rock face.) The creek cascades another 8 to 10', split into three streams. Its waters slide into a small pool. The creek then flows under the bridge and over smooth bedrock to form a set of lower falls. The lower falls should be avoided because of the slick rock and dangerous drop-off. Below the lower falls the creek tumbles through a jumble of boulders and down the cove, disappearing into the woods.

Laurel Falls is best photographed in the early morning, before the sun rises over its right side, or on an overcast day.

2. Huskey Branch Cascades

Roads: Paved   A "4"
USGS Quadrangle: Gatlinburg, TN
Little River Trail, 2.1 miles, easy

Directions: Take the Elkmont Campground access road. Prior to the campground entrance (1.45 miles) turn left. Cross the Little River at 2.1 miles. The parking area lies just ahead, where the road forks.

From the parking area, hike the Little River Trail (a paved road) which leads left (southeast) passing through an old resort community (the buildings and

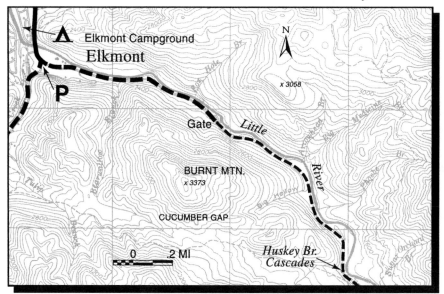

grounds are off limits). At just under a quarter mile the paved treadway gives way to gravel. Ascending at an easy rate alongside the Little River, at .55 of a mile the roadbed bends right and momentarily distances itself from the river. Nearing the one-mile point, arrive at a turnaround with a signed gate stating, "Road Closed." (This is the old trailhead.)

The road serving as the trail continues its easy ascent up the Little River drainage. Beneath the north and east slopes of Burnt Mountain, for the next mile or so, the trail is at times near the river, then at others distant, while passing through a hardwood-dominated forest. Plants and flowers seen along the route, include: bloodroot; ferns; foamflower; jack-in-the-pulpit; showy orchis; white violets; yellow trillium; and dense rhododendron.

At 2.1 miles arrive at the footbridge crossing, and trailside viewing area of the Huskey Branch Cascades.

This is a triple cascade with a total height of approximately 15'. In a run of 60', the creek has cut a 3'-deep channel in the rock. The surrounding bedrock is covered in the most beautiful, gold-tinged, emerald-green moss. The dark underlying rock deepens the green.

3. The Sinks

A "2"
No hiking map needed.

From the parking area, hike the Meigs Creek Trail due south. In 130' arrive at the viewing area of this broader than high cascade.

The Little River enters the scene as rapids rushing under the Little River Road bridge. Gaining force and speed, its status changes to that of a cascade as the waters churn over a rugged, 8', bedrock outcrop. Its main flow, channeled over the right side, flows clear with a slight green tint. The lesser flow, on the left, is foaming white. At their base the river boils in a pool of unseen depths. Like sparkling water, the pool's bubbles escape with a fizz. Constricted by bedrock, the river exits the pool in a slow and deep foaming flow.

4. Meigs Falls

A "2"
Seen from a roadside pullout.

This waterfall is seen from a pullout on the left (south) side of Little River Road. The falls lie across the river and approximately 400' up Meigs Creek (a tributary that joins the Little River here).

To get good photos of this waterfall you'll need *at least* a 300mm lens and even lighting.

5. The Intersection of Laurel Creek Road (the Townsend Wye) as above.

Gatlinburg Area
(Roaring Fork Motor Nature Trail)

Directions: The distances given below are cumulative and begin at traffic light #8 on US 441, in downtown Gatlinburg.

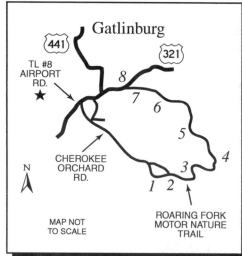

Note: The Roaring Fork Motor Nature Trail (RFMNT), which accesses points 2 through 6, is gated during wintry conditions.

Zero your odometer at traffic light #8 and head east on Airport Road. In .65 of a mile veer right onto Cherokee Orchard Road. At 2.8 miles the road forks. You must now veer right, as the route is one-way. The following points of interest are accessed on this 10-mile loop:

1. Rainbow Falls - Bullhead trails parking area: 3.4 miles.
2. The Roaring Fork Motor Nature Trail begins: 3.75 miles.
3. Upper access Baskins Creek Trail: 3.95 miles. (See item #5, below.)
4. Grotto Falls parking: 5.45 miles.
5. Lower access Baskins Creek Trail *(#10 stop on RFMNT, near Jim Bales Place)*: 6.75 miles. (See item #3, above.)
6. The Place of a Thousand Drips: 8.7 miles.
7. Low Gap Road (stop sign): 9.3 miles.
8. US 321 in Gatlinburg: 10 miles.

1. Rainbow Falls

Roads: Paved   A "10"
#2 stop on the Roaring Fork Motor Nature Trail
USGS Quadrangle: Mt. Le Conte, TN, NC
Rainbow Falls Trail, 2.7 miles. Allow at least 1/2 day.
Difficult: Rocky treadway, some steep grades, minor water crossings

---

At this location look for the trailhead on the southwest side of the parking area, at a sign stating, "Rainbow Falls Trail, Trillium Gap Trail .1 mile, Rainbow Falls 2.7 miles." Other destinations are listed, as well.

The trail enters the woods and soon bends left. At 110' stay left while passing by a confusing split to the right. With a slight right bend, at 260', the trail tops out. At 355' intersect the Trillium Gap Trail. A sign states, "Rainbow Falls Trail, Rainbow Falls, 2.6 miles." Again, other routes and destinations are pointed out, as well.

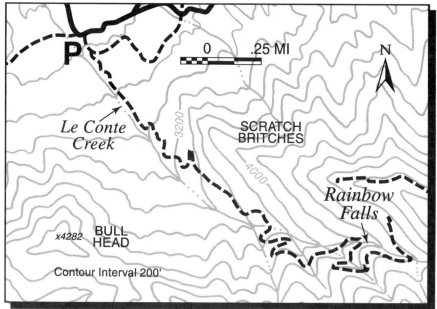

Heading towards Rainbow Falls, the trail winds while ascending through beautiful, moss- and lichen-covered boulders and at 600' arrives beside Le Conte Creek. Amongst the boulders, massive chestnut stumps and fallen logs attest to the presence of this once great tree. At 800' the trail turns left and ascends a rocky point of land with Le Conte Creek rushing by on the right. Leveling for the moment, at .35 of a mile, the trail once again draws near the creek. (This portion of the Rainbow Falls Trail treads a great deal of rubble. However, many of the larger boulders have been moved aside to facilitate hiking.) At .55 of a mile the trail makes a noticeable left turn and switchbacks up the mountain. Meandering through the rocky woodland, over wet spots, but to the dry side of the ridge line, at .85 of a mile near the creek once again (which is 150' away and unseen from this point). At just over a mile, with a left (north) turn, the trail makes an ascent across the lower slopes of Scratch Britches. Arriving at a point of land (1.15 miles) the trail makes a hard right and levels somewhat. After passing beautiful rock outcrops, to the trail's left side, once again ascend over rock and roots. At 1.55 miles enter a stand of large trees whose understory is littered with boulders. In this woodland boulderfield cross two wet-weather branches and note the abundance of Fraser's sedge. The trail soon rejoins Le Conte Creek which is now approximately 40' below trail level. Heading upstream, the treadway levels atop a stacked rock buildup. At 1.85 miles cross a small, wet-weather branch. Soon thereafter, enter an area of large boulders where the trail turns sharply right to cross scenic Le Conte Creek on a footlog-type footbridge.

The trail now begins its steep, switchbacking ascent of a finger ridge between Le Conte Creek and an unnamed tributary to its southwest. The outstanding feature on this leg of the hike is the massive hemlocks, some with a circumference of 15'. The next landmark (2.4 miles) is an unnamed tributary of Le Conte Creek with a small, trailside waterfall. Trillium and ferns abound on its banks.

Crossing this branch on steppingstones, the trail then ascends, briefly levels, bends right, and soon crosses a lesser tributary. Soon thereafter, amongst heavy boulders, cross Le Conte Creek on the second footlog. Upon crossing, the trail turns left then sharply right and at 2.7 miles arrives at the third footlog and viewing area for Rainbow Falls. A closer view of the falls may be had by clambering up the rubble-like boulders on the left side of the creek. (The Rainbow Falls Trail continues across the footlog, onward to Mt. Le Conte.)

This veil-like fall spills 83' from the ledge of a 400'-wide cirque that has been undercut by weathering. In its spray zone Kelly-green mosses thrive. Rock tripe and light green and yellow colored lichens have colonized the drier rock. The lichen-covered cirque is an awesome patchwork of greens and grays streaked vertically with the browns of algaes and tannin. The cove is littered with large boulders. Heavy talus, at the base of the cirque, provides shelter for the not-too-shy, resident ground squirrels. Grotesquely crooked trees at the base lend an eerie beauty to the setting.

Rainbow Falls is best photographed early in the morning or on a cloudy day.

2. The Roaring Fork Motor Nature Trail (as above).

3. & 5. Baskins Creek Falls

(Actually located on Falls Branch.)

Roads: Paved   A "5"
USGS Quadrangle: Mt. Le Conte, TN, NC
1.7 miles via Upper Trail & 1.6 miles via Lower Trail, minor water crossings,
difficult

---

3. Via the Upper Baskins Creek Trail

Note: This is what I consider the back way in to this waterfall. Since it is the first route to this waterfall encountered on the Roaring Fork Motor Nature Trail, it is listed accordingly. I prefer the Lower Baskins Creek Trail (see below).

At this location look for the parking area on the right. The trail begins 75' ahead, on the left side of the RFMNT. There may be a sign stating, "Baskins Creek Trail," with other destinations listed, as well.

The trail enters the hardwood forest and leads level for 220', then with a right turn descends into a small hollow. Undulating while winding, at 490' cross a small branch flowing through a stone culvert. The trail now meanders while

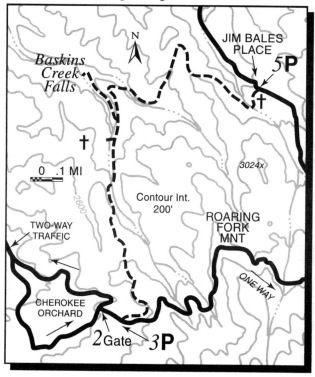

ascending and outlining the high end of a couple of small coves. At .2 of a mile the trail turns sharply left (northwesterly) and levels off on the mountainside (much like a contour line). Between .25 and .3 of a mile there are through-the-trees views of the mountains to the south. At .35 of a mile, with a hollow to the west, pass alongside the crest of the ridge. After more open views, cross the ridge through a saddle.

Now on the east slope, with a hollow to your right, the trail trends north while descending the crest of a ridge. At .55 of a mile the trail enters a rhododendron thicket and soon levels. In .1 of a mile the trail descends once again. Three fourths of a mile into the hike the trail bends right, leaving the ridge line, and descends more steeply. The sounds of Falls Branch are now heard through the rhododendron. At just over .9 of a mile, the trail makes a noticeable bend right and descends in switchback fashion to cross Falls Branch on steppingstones. Now on the creek's east side, the route turns sharply left and heads downstream. At the 1 mile point pass a prominent, rock overhang. As the hollow widens the trail trends away from the creek and soon treads a point of land between Falls Branch and an unnamed branch on the right. At 1.2 miles pass a side path on the left. This leads south for 715' to the Baskins Cemetery. The main trail bends north at this location. After crossing a small branch, wind through the rhododendron and cross the previously mentioned unnamed branch on steppingstones (just above its confluence with Falls Branch). The trail now continues through a hemlock thicket, which soon gives way to rhododendron, as it follows Falls Branch downstream. At 1.4 miles arrive at the Fall's Trail, which is on the left (see below)*. (At the time of my hike this side trail was unmarked.)

5. Via the Lower Baskins Creek Trail
The trail enters the woods leading due west from the parking area, and initially treads level through a forest of hemlock and small hardwoods with ferns filling the understory. In 240', while passing by the Ogle, Bales, Reagan Cemetery, the trail turns left and starts descending. In a right bend, at 475', cross a small stream flowing through a rock culvert. Exiting the hollow's depths, the trail treads level while heading northwesterly, then at 700' begins a rather steep ascent. Topping out (.45 of a mile) leave the shaded forest for a more open woodland, along the crest of a ridge. Heading northerly, first level, then slightly descending, at .55 of a mile the rate of descent steepens. With a sharp left turn, at .6 of a mile, the trail narrows as it leaves the ridge crest to tread the bottom of a ravine. The sounds of a small brook soon become evident as the trail makes a long bend right, passing in and out of the rhododendron. At just over a mile this brook joins Baskins Creek. After a short muddy stretch, the trail turns sharply left to cross Baskins Creek (1.15 miles). (Prior to this crossing there is a confusing pathway leading downstream. *Do not take it!*) The trail now turns steeply uphill, tops a ridge and descends. At just over 1.3 miles the trail levels in a fern-filled, bog-like opening. After passing over the old roadbed's stone fill, through which the bog drains, the trail reenters the woods. Twenty paces from the stone fill, look for the Fall's Trail which leads *right* (north northwest, see below)*. (At the time of my hike this side trail was unmarked.) The Baskins Creek Trail continues straight ahead from this point. (See Upper Baskins Creek Trail, above.)

*Fall's Trail

The Fall's Trail immediately enters dense woods which soon give way to a fern-filled opening. Doghobble and rhododendron are encountered as the trail joins Falls Branch. Soon, the trail crosses a wet-weather branch and treads a soggy stretch. At .2 of a mile the trail ascends and with a right bend rounds a rocky point. *Beware of the precipice on the left.* While descending, at just under a quarter mile, turn sharply left to enter the fall's cirque. Soon thereafter, arrive at the base of the falls.

This very beautiful waterfall spills from a massive, 400'-wide, sandstone cirque. The cliff's left side is approximately 35'high, its right side is 25'higher than the sloping earth below. A small spout of water falls 150' to the right of the main waterfall. Falls Branch flows through a channel cut in the sandstone and spills 25'in two tiers. The sandstone is block-like and several large chunks have fallen away from the cliffs. One large boulder is positioned directly in front of the falls and obscures the view, somewhat. Driftwood and waterborne logs hang up on boulders and a small island at its base.

From the base, the creek flows to the left then exits the scene as cascades. The rock is the main attraction here. In and around the falls deep green mosses cover much of it.

This location best photographs in the early morning or late evening. An overcast day would be a good time, as well, as the beautiful rock is evenly lit.

4. Grotto Falls

Roads: Paved   A "4" 20'
Stop #5 on the Roaring Fork Motor Nature Trail
USGS Quadrangle: Mt. Le Conte, TN, NC
Trillium Gap Trail, 1.3 miles, minor water crossings, moderate

At this location, what I call the "Trillium Gap Connector" begins just past the east end of the parking area. A sign at the trailhead states, "Trillium Gap Trail, Grotto Falls 1.2 miles." Other destinations are listed, as well.

The trail initially passes through a forest dominated by hemlock. In 85' an access from the overflow parking area intersects from the left. Ascending, while meandering through the woods, at 420' cross a small, wet-weather branch. At .15 of a mile bisect the Trillium Gap Trail. A sign points the way towards the falls (left) and to other destinations, as well. Running level, the trail soon crosses a small creek on steppingstones. With a sharp left bend, the trail ascends. Leveling at the quarter mile, arrive at an open point of land where the trail turns sharply right. For the next .85 of a mile ascend moderately over many rocky and root-laced stretches, while outlining flower-filled hollows, and crossing small creeks and ridge

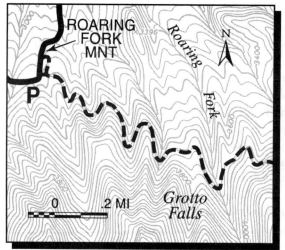

lines. Topping out, at 1.1 miles, the treadway levels while entering the cove of Grotto Falls. The lower falls soon become visible. In passing, notice the tilted shale exposure on the right. After treading an especially rocky stretch, arrive at the upper tier of Grotto Falls (1.3 miles).

At the time of my hike the fall's cove was littered with storm damage. The flowway above the upper falls was filled with downed treetops.

Housed in a U-shaped cirque, of sorts, this 15', free falling waterfall has a total height of 20', counting the small cascades above it. The creek has cut a deep channel into the rock from which it falls. The falls are of the caprock variety, as they are undercutting the sandstone. Its waters splash onto the rock below and flow into a small, blue-green pool. Green and gold-green mosses thrive on the rock to the left side of the falls. Make a dry pass behind them for a view from the east side.

A very popular destination, visit Grotto Falls early in the morning to avoid the crowds. While Grotto Falls is teeming with visitors, nearby Baskins Creek Falls won't have a soul.

Flowers seen here, include: bellwort, Fraser's sedge, squirrel corn, trillium, and trout lily.

5. Lower access Baskins Creek Falls (see pgs. 17 and 18).

6. The Place of a Thousand Drips

Stop #15 on the RFMNT. Moss thickly covers the rock of this wet-weather wonder. During dry times, thousands of small trickles are prevalent here, thus its name. For a real show, see them after heavy spring rains.

7. Low Gap Road (as above).

8. US 321 in Gatlinburg (as above).

Greenbrier Area

Directions: From the intersection of US Hwys. 441 and 321 (the #3 traffic light) in Gatlinburg, drive north on US 321 for 6.1 miles to the park's

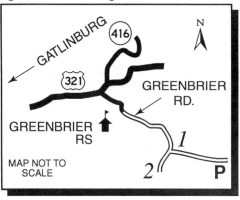

Greenbrier entrance (Greenbrier Road). Turn right (south) and drive the following distances to access these points of interest:

1. Middle Prong Road (access to the Ramsay Cascades): 3.2 miles.

2. The parking area for Fern Branch Falls (accessed via the Porters Creek Trail): 4.1 miles.

1. The Ramsay Cascades

Roads: Graveled   A "10+"
USGS Quadrangle: Mt. Guyot, TN, NC
4 miles, water crossings, difficult   Allow 6 to 8 hours.

Of the more than 350 waterfalls that I've visited, this one ranks at the top.

Note: Be prepared for cooler temperatures. It may be 10 to 15° cooler at the falls than at the trailhead.

Directions: From Greenbrier Road, take Middle Prong Road for 1.55 miles to trail parking. The trail begins at the jeep-blocking boulders 125' east (upstream) of the parking lot.

With a left bend, at 215', cross the Middle Prong of the Little Pigeon River on a single-lane footbridge. Now on the river's north side, with a right turn the trail heads upstream, ascending at an easy to moderate rate. This soon changes to a more moderate ascent after passing by large boulders on both the left and right sides of the trail. The next notable feature is a sharp left bend at the quarter-mile. One third of a mile into the hike, pass through a boulder field. Boulders found here range in size from that of a room to a small house. At .7 of a mile listen carefully for a gurgling, underground brook. When I first heard its earthen echoes (which sounded like crackling gravel) I thought that I was being overtaken by a vehicle. At .8 of a mile the roadbed tops out then descends for the first time and soon levels amongst beds of crested dwarf iris. In places, the flower's greenery is as thick as a fescue lawn. Between 1.25 and 1.3 miles cross three branches in quick succession, the last being Ramsay Branch, which is crossed via a footbridge. At 1.4 miles the trail closely approaches Middle Prong, within 20' of the river, but some 30-40' in elevation above it.

One and five-tenths miles into the hike reach a circular turnaround. The trail is routed to the left here. While rounding the circle's left side, pass the faint, Greenbrier Pinnacle Trail (shown on the quadrangle as an old jeep road) which departs with a sharp left. Upon reaching the circle's apex look for a sign stating, "Ramsay Cascades Trail, Ramsay Cascade 2.5."

Narrowing to a single track, while entering the drainage of Ramsay Prong, the trail often passes through tunnels of rhododendron and over rock and roots while ascending at a moderate rate. Meandering, with an undulating ascent, at times within eyesight of the stream, at 1.85 miles the treadway levels momentarily, in the midst of some rather large hemlock. At 2 miles, with one step, cross a small brook (possibly dry in the summer). Continuing upstream, the trail ascends to a point 50' above Ramsay Prong. At 2.1 miles descend, and with a single bound cross another small creek. The view of Ramsay Prong is awesome in this area. Especially beautiful is the undercut rock wall on the south side of the creek. The trail descends, bends in reverse "S" fashion while passing through the creek's overflow area, and at 2.15 miles crosses Ramsay Prong on a footlog-type footbridge. Again, the views, both up and down-stream, are awesome.

The trail now narrows significantly as we enter virgin timber territory. Ascending over a very rocky stretch, the treadway soon levels and rejoins the creek, winding alongside it. Two and three-tenths miles into the hike, begin a more moderate to difficult ascent while passing gigantic beech, hemlock, and mountain magnolias. At 2.55 miles the trail bends left, then right, winding through a stand of virgin poplar with trillium as a ground cover. After a brief view of the creek, the trail once again starts uphill through rock and over roots. At 2.7 miles, while passing alongside Ramsay Prong's overflow area, the trail ascends at a more difficult rate. (The rocky treadway makes an otherwise moderate ascent a difficult one. After rainfall, much of this portion of the trail takes on the status of a creek.) The next landmark is a large, 12 by 20' split boulder. The trail passes to the stream side of this boulder, and just out of the overflow area, while treading over heavy rock. At 2.9 miles ascend inground rock steps with a cave-like, rock overhang to the trail's right side. Just ahead, the trail tops out then bends left to cross Ramsay Prong on a footlog footbridge. The view of the stream from this bridge is unbelievably beautiful—a colorful kaleidoscope of greens, browns, golds, and grays, with splashes of whitewater flowing between the boulders.

Once again, tread over roots, rock, and rock steps, now on the north side of the boulder-filled, tumbling creek. At 3.15 miles cross a small branch on steppingstones, then in 50' a larger one. Prevalent in this vicinity is a small tree known as witch-hobble. Its white blooms remind me of Queen Anne's lace, but on a larger scale. From this point, the trail crosses and recrosses several

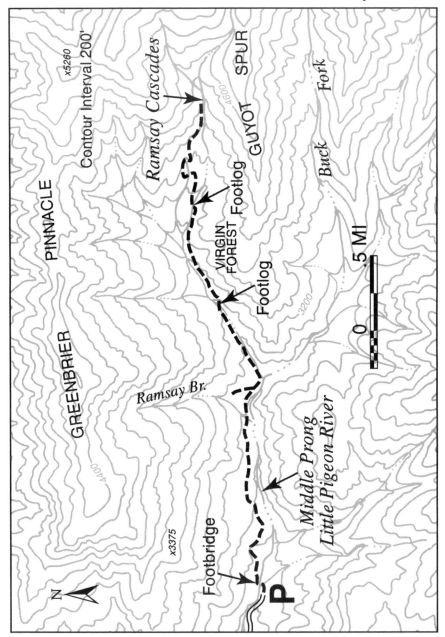

tributary branches then at 3.3 miles heads northerly. Treading the west slope of the mountainside for a short distance, the trail then turns easterly. In the vicinity of 3.5 miles, through the open woods to the south, the sloping, fir-topped ridge of Guyot Spur is visible. The trail winds while ascending over heavy rubble-like rock, rock steps, and roots, then at 3.75 miles treads over and through heavy boulders and downed timbers (within 50' of Ramsay Prong's main flow). While not in the stream's course, one would think otherwise after heavy rainfall. Peeks at the beautiful, boulder-filled stream are offered along an especially tough stretch (3.8 miles), as the trail either treads over heavy boulders or winds through them. At 4 miles cross a tributary of Ramsay Prong on boulders and steppingstones. Continue upstream for another 200' to the fall's viewing area.

Rising on the rugged, west slopes of Mt. Guyot and Old Black Mtn., Ramsay Prong's waters careen from ledge to ledge in a fall of 50'. Its sandstone rock face has been fissured by weathering. Landing on conglomerate sandstone bedrock, crisscrossed with quartz veins, its swift waters collect briefly in a small pool where they take on a light green tint. The creek then slides and cascades downstream. A bright green algae grows on the moist bedrock with a small amount of moss growing where periodically moistened. On drier rock, rock tripe thrives. A large jumble of boulders on the left side, at the base, provides a viewing point.

The Ramsay Cascades are best photographed in the late afternoon, when fully sunlit. The even lighting of an overcast day also works well.

2. Fern Branch Falls

Roads: Graveled   A "4" 35'
USGS Quadrangle: Mt. Le Conte, TN, NC
1.85 miles, water crossings, moderate

This hike features some of the most diverse and prolific wildflower displays in the park.

A sign at the trailhead (gate) states, "Porters Creek Trail," with distances for various destinations given.

From the parking area the trail treads a graveled road, beginning its undulating ascent of the Porters Creek drainage. At .35 of a mile cross a culverted branch and soon thereafter a small branch on steppingstones. At .65 of a mile the careful observer will notice a stacked rock wall, on the right, with carefully laid steps leading up to an old homestead. The ruins of a fireplace lie 125' off the main trail, here. At .7 of a mile pass another stacked rock wall to the trail's right. At just under .75 of a mile cross Long Branch (a rather large tributary) on a wooden bridge. Soon thereafter, pass by steps leading up the slope to a hilltop cemetery. As the trail levels (.8 of a mile), look for an old car rusting away in the woods 125' to the trail's right. In a left bend (.85 of a mile) cross a footlog footbridge over an unnamed tributary. The trail soon passes through a hardwood and hemlock forest with a meandering ascent. At .95 of a mile arrive at a point where the roadbed splits. Continue straight ahead (the left route) on the Porters Creek Trail. (The route on the right accesses the

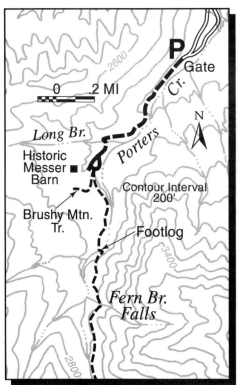

Brushy Mountain Trail and the historic, Messer farm site.)

Just ahead, after leveling, the trail makes a potentially confusing split. Continue straight here, as well, and at the 1 mile point a path from the historic farm site intersects from the right. (The treadway is now narrower, as the graveled road ends in the vicinity of the farm site.) Distant from Porters Creek, at 1.2 miles pass a large sandstone boulder (on the left) with a 1/4" wide band of quartz running through it. Soon leveling, pass several large boulders to the right side of the trail and a large, rotting hemlock stump (1.45 miles). The trail makes a reverse "S" here and crosses a footlog footbridge over Porters Creek.

This is a very beautiful creek—crystal clear with multicolored rock and boulders lining its course. The creek takes on a tint of green in its foaming, frothy waters.

The trail now turns east and heads downstream then soon bends right to once again head in a southerly direction (upstream). Narrowing to a single track, the trail ascends at a more moderate rate. One and six-tenths miles into the hike pass a gigantic poplar (to the trail's left). This tree (if still standing) is at least 10' in circumference. From this point, the treadway becomes very rocky. Meandering while ascending, at just over 1.8 miles the fall's delicate rush becomes heard. At 1.85 miles cross Fern Branch on steppingstones. The falls are seen approximately 150' upstream.

This 35' waterfall is aptly named for its abundance of ferns. There is a massive cliff to their left side with a rock overhang. In the foreground lies a very large boulder which is split into thirds. Moss is plentiful here, as is wild stonecrop. Below the falls the creek cascades through hundreds of small boulders and lush aquatic vegetation.

Fern Branch Falls photographs best in the early morning before the sun clears the top of the mountain behind it, or on an overcast day.

Cosby Area

Henwallow Falls

Roads: Paved   An "8"
USGS Quadrangle: Hartford, TN, NC
Gabes Mountain Trail, 2.3 miles, moderate

Directions: From the intersection of US 321 and TN 32 in Cosby (18.5 miles

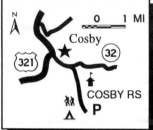

east of Gatlinburg), drive east on 32 for 1.2 miles to the Great Smoky Mountains, Cosby access. Turn right (south). In 2 miles look for the Gabes Mountain Trail (the route to the falls), on the right. Trail parking is just ahead (2.1 miles from TN 32) at the *second* parking area on the left.

The trail (which we passed on the inbound road) begins 175' north of the first picnic area access, and enters the woods to the west. A sign at the trailhead states, "Gabes Mountain Trail, Henwallow Falls 2.2," with other destinations listed, as well.

Upon entering the woods, the trail ascends at a moderate rate over rock and roots, passing through a predominately hardwood forest. Sounds of a rushing stream, to the trail's right, soon break the silence. At just under a quarter mile the trail turns southwesterly and continues its ascent. Three tenths of a mile into the hike, the campground access trail intersects from the left. (Signs give directions and distances.) The fall's trail bends right, then left, and heads towards the very audible Rock Creek. Cross this creek at .35 of a mile on a footlog footbridge. Soon after crossing, the trail turns upstream once again. From this point the trail crosses several small ridges and tributaries of Rock and Crying creeks. After crossing the main tributary of Crying Creek

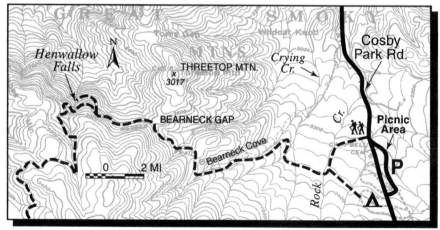

(the third footlog, just over .7 of a mile) the trail turns northerly, then meanders west to ascend Bearneck Cove at a more moderate rate. The sounds of a creek soon resonate through the laurel, on the right. At the 1 mile point, the trail levels for a short distance then descends into the hollow of this creek, soon crossing it on a double-culverted stone bridge. Ascending out of the creek in a westerly direction, intersect then tread an old roadbed while crossing a woodland opening. At the upper end of the opening the road ends in cul-de-sac fashion (1.05 miles). (At this location trail signs point out the various routes.) The trail now reenters the woods and heads generally west, often within earshot of the last-crossed creek, while ascending at a moderate and progressively more difficult rate. At 1.25 miles the trail bends north to trace the high end of Bearneck Cove. Ascending, while passing under a canopy of rhododendron, crest a saddle (1.4 miles). (A side path leads east to its high point.)

The trail now trends northwesterly, paralleling the slopes of an upland hollow that opens to the northeast. The treadway now becomes more conducive to hiking (not as rocky and rooty). While descending, at 1.55 miles, cross a small branch flowing through a rock culvert. With a right turn the trail ascends and soon passes under a canopy of rhododendron and hemlock. Top the saddle of Bearneck Gap at 1.75 miles, whereupon the trail bends westerly to continue its ascent. After outlining a sharp, but shallow, rhododendron-filled hollow, pass massive boulders (seen on the left) and cross a small branch flowing under the roadbed. After passing another major boulder outcrop, the trail makes an undulating ascent and arrives at the Henwallow Falls side trail (2.15 miles).

The fall's trail descends steeply, rounding the east and north slopes of a ridge, while entering the hollow of Lower Falling Branch. At 2.3 miles arrive at the fall's viewing area.

This low-volume waterfall is of the sliding variety. Approximately 4' wide, the creek spills over the edge and fans out to a width of 10'. The sandstone bedrock flanking its sides is covered in emerald-green mosses. Jack-in-the-pulpit and a wide variety of ferns thrive in its moist environs. Colorful sandstone talus litters the base.

Big Creek Area

Mouse Creek Falls

Roads: Graveled   An "8"
USGS Quadrangles: Luftee Knob, Cove Creek Gap, NC, TN
Big Creek Trail, 2 miles, minor water crossings, easy-moderate

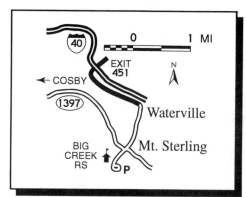

Directions: From the intersection of US 321 and TN 32 in Cosby, Tennessee, drive east on 32. In 11.2 miles the pavement ends and the road's designation changes to SR 1397 as you enter North Carolina. Drive another 1.2 miles (12.4 total from Cosby) to a 4-way intersection in the community of Mt. Sterling, North Carolina. Turn right. *Enter the Great Smoky Mountains National Park, and in .25 of a mile pass the Big Creek ranger station. Continuing, at .85 of a mile, in a left bend, look for the gated, Big Creek Trail, which is on the right. Trail parking is located just ahead at the campground/picnic parking area.

Alternate directions: If traveling I-40 from Asheville or Knoxville, take the Waterville Exit (Exit 451) and follow the signs for 2.2 miles to the Big Creek access, which is straight ahead. (*See directions above.)

From the parking entry/exit point, walk the entrance road north for 165′ to the Big Creek Trail (previously mentioned), on the left.

From the gate, the Big Creek Trail bends right then left and in 125′ straightens. Ascending while heading generally southwest, the trail parallels the unseen Big Creek at a distance of 300 to 400′. At 685′ cross a culvert with a deep hollow to its right. The next landmark, a side path on the left (.2 of a mile), descends in ramp-like fashion, heading towards the campground. At the quarter mile, Big Creek becomes visible far below (approximately 60′ below trail level) through the open woods. Green mosses, gray lichens, firepink, and wild stonecrop thrive on the roadbed's many sandstone cuts. At .45 of a mile the observant hiker will notice a midstream island far below trail level. At .65 of a mile cross a small, rocky, wet-weather branch whose culvert consists of a concrete pipe and rock headwall. In this area moss-covered logs stand out in brilliant green against the browns of the forest floor. At .95 of a mile pass a large and scenic boulder-covered slope to the trail's right. Amongst these beautiful boulders, at just over a mile, an old roadbed intersects in ramp fashion, from the right. Notable at 1.2 miles, are massive boulders in the creek's overflow area. A scant landmark, known as the "Rock House," lies approximately 200′ up a steep side path in this vicinity. Early settlers used its natural shelter as a temporary homeplace. Trailside boulders soon diminish and give way to the next landmark—Big Creek's Midnight Hole. This wondrous sight is accessed via a short side path at 1.45 miles.

Big Creek's entirety is channeled through an 8′ opening in the boulders forming a 6′ cascade that spills into a bottomless, blue-green pool. The rock wall to its left makes this already beautiful spot even more so.

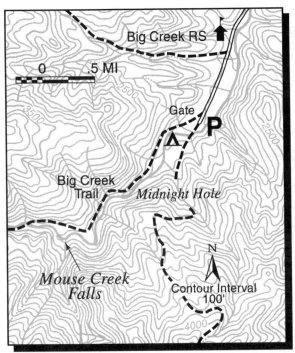

Back on the main trail, at 1.55 miles, look for a small landslide to the trail's right. Just ahead, look for a straight, white-water stretch of creek with a view of .1 of a mile, or more, upstream. With a sharp right bend, at 1.7 miles, leave sight of the creek. As trail and creek rejoin, an especially scenic view of its boulder-filled course is presented. At 2 miles the main trail veers right. (A side path at this location leads left to a hitching post.) In 65' look for a slim side path leading 100' to the viewing area of Mouse Creek Falls.

Flowing directly into Big Creek, this cascading-type waterfall is approximately 30' high. The upper tier is approximately 20' high. Pooling, Mouse Creek then runs 10 to 15' and tumbles another 8' into Big Creek. Big Creek eddies a frothy, green-white foam at their base as its waters lap at midstream bedrock. The setting is beautifully framed by hemlock and rhododendron, on both the near and far sides of the creek.

Twentymile Area

Twentymile Cascades

See Snowbird - Tapoco Area pgs. 40 and 50.

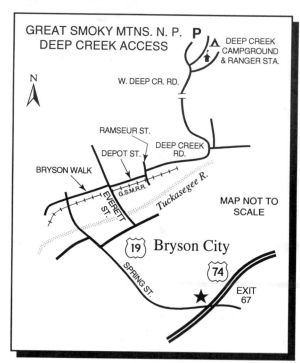

GREAT SMOKY MTNS. N. P.
DEEP CREEK ACCESS

P

DEEP CREEK
CAMPGROUND
& RANGER STA.

W. DEEP CR. RD.

N

RAMSEUR ST.

DEPOT ST.

DEEP CREEK
RD.

BRYSON WALK

G.S.M.R.R.

EVERETT ST.

Tuckasegee R.

MAP NOT TO
SCALE

19 Bryson City

74

SPRING ST.

EXIT
67

Bryson City - Deep Creek Area

Directions: Traveling US 74, take Exit 67 (the Bryson City Exit) and follow the signs to the Great Smoky Mountains, Deep Creek access.

Juney Whank Falls

Roads: Graveled   A "3"
USGS Quadrangle: Bryson City, NC
.3 of a mile, moderate-difficult See Tom's Branch for hiking map.

The fall's trail begins across Juney Whank Branch, south of the Deep Creek Trail parking area. There may be jeep-blocking boulders at the trailhead, as well as a sign denoting the trail.

The trail enters the woods and ascends at a moderate rate. At 260' a path leads right as the main trail turns sharply left to ascend the mountainside. At 460' a trail (an old roadbed) used by pack stock joins from the left. The trail is now both a hiker and horse trail. The route makes a hard right here. In the area around 500' the trail bends left to round the foot of a ridge. Continuing its ascent, enter then outline a small hollow. At .2 of a mile the trail bends left at a point of land to enter the fall's hollow. The falls are soon heard. At the quarter mile look for a side trail leading to their base. Take this descending side trail for 145' to the fall's viewing area (a footlog footbridge over Juney Whank Branch).

The main portion of Juney Whank is approximately 40' high, falling in 5 to 6 tiers. The creek enters the scene as a 2 to 3'-wide flow which spills 3', splashing and broadening to 8'. With a slide down bedrock, the falls fan out to a width of 12 to 15′ at the base. The creek then cascades down the mountainside to join Deep Creek.

The side trail continues east and ties back into the horse trail in another 235′. This route *does* lead back to the parking area, but hiking it is not advised as it eventually treads a slick wash enroute to the Deep Creek Trail.

Tom's Branch and Indian Creek Falls

A "2" & A "5" respectively
USGS Quadrangle: Bryson City, NC
Deep Creek and Indian Creek trails, .25 and .8 of a mile respectively,
easy-moderate

The Deep Creek Trail (the route to Tom's Branch and Indian Creek Falls) treads the gated, logging railroad bed that enters the woods to the left side of the Deep Creek Trail parking area.

At the outset the trail is rated easy, rising gently then descending. One-fourth mile into the hike arrive at Tom's Branch Falls.

Lying across, and spilling directly into Deep Creek, the falls are approximately 60′ high, consisting of 4 major tiers. To be assured of adequate water, visit this waterfall in the wet months. Laurel and hardwoods flank its sides and overhang to somewhat shroud them from view. In spring, they're made more beautiful when the surrounding dogwoods are in bloom.

Tom's Branch best photographs in the early morning with the sun behind the ridge, or on an overcast day.

Continuing upstream, the trail makes a gradual left bend and soon bends right to cross Deep Creek on a footbridge (.4 of a mile). The trail then bends right, in harmony with the creek, to round the foot of a ridge. Nearing the half-mile point, begin a more moderate ascent. Travel soon becomes much easier as the route levels then descends more closely to creek level. Three fourths of a mile into the hike, with a footbridge lying straight ahead, arrive at the junction of the Indian Creek Trail. (A sign states, "Indian Creek Trail, Indian Creek Falls 200′," with other destinations listed, as well.)

The Indian Creek Trail leads to the right (east) while ascending at a moderate rate. Eight tenths of a mile into the hike arrive at the Indian Creek Fall's side trail. Descend the rocky (and at times muddy) side trail and in 80' arrive at the viewing area at the base.

Entering the scene as cascades, this 20'-wide, 20'-high, foaming-white, sliding-type waterfall is fully broken—there is no smooth flow. During periods of low water its flow would be split in half. The fall makes a bubbly entry into a deep pool that is surrounded by rhododendron. The creek exits the pool over small, water-smoothed rocks.

Several varieties of ferns and trillium, as well as foamflower and star chickweed crowd the slopes near the base. Other area flora, include: crested dwarf iris, wild geranium, blue and white violets, jack-in-the-pulpit, and showy orchis.

This waterfall is best photographed on a cloudy day.

Cherokee Area

Note: This area is provided with two Area Maps, please see below and pg. 34.

Little Creek Falls

Roads: Graveled   An "8"
USGS Quadrangles: Smokemont, Whittier, NC, in their margins.
Cooper Creek & Deeplow Gap trails, 1.45 miles, minor water crossings*,
moderate

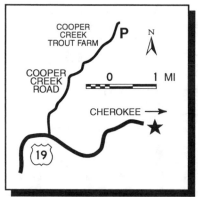

Note: For the first quarter mile the route treads a graveled road passing through private land. Please do not deviate from this road.

Directions: From the intersection of US Hwys. 19 and 441, west of Cherokee, drive south on US 19 for 5.15 miles to Cooper Creek Road (SR 1355). Turn right and travel 3.4 miles to the Cooper Creek Trout Farm parking area, which is on the right. The trout farm owners, the Crocketts, have been kind enough to let us park and pass: please respect their property so that we may be invited back.

From the north end of the parking area, hike the private road north and in 450' veer right on a one-lane graveled road. At 650' pass by a barn, which is on the left. In just over 100' the road passes the trout farm's water intake and

32

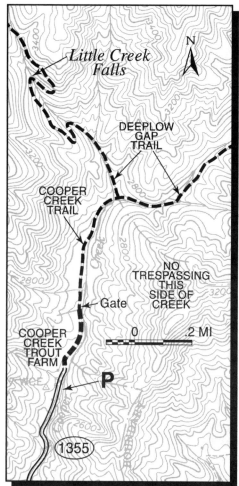

enters the woods. At the quarter mile enter the national park and soon thereafter arrive at a turn-around, gate, and the Cooper Creek Trailhead. The trail (the continuing roadbed) runs level within 30 to 40' of its namesake. Just ahead, pass by *very* private property, which lies to the east side of Cooper Creek. From all of the no trespassing signs, and from what I'm told, this landowner dislikes outsiders. *The trail is flooded for the next 500 to 600'. Hikers have taken several meandering wood-land routes, to the trail's left, to avoid the ankle- to boot-deep wa-ters of Cooper Creek. On dry land once again, at the half mile, we resume our unhampered passage. Three fourths of a mile into the hike, at a ford, the trail makes a minor left and right jog to cross Little Creek on a footlog. In 135' intersect the Deeplow Gap Trail, which continues both *straight*, up Cooper Creek, and *left*, towards the falls.

The trail ascends the Little Creek drainage at a moderate rate. After crossing several wet-weather tribu-taries, cross a footlog over Little Creek (1.1 miles). This is a beautiful spot, with mossy rocks, and an abundance of bluets and foamflower. In crossing Little Creek, the trail turns to the left to ascend in switchback fashion. On the higher and drier slopes, at 1.2 miles, the trail bends right. Low-growing plants, such as Catesby's trillium, maidenhair fern, and *poison ivy*, crowd the now narrow treadway. After having hiked 1.45 miles arrive at the footlog crossing/viewing area of Little Creek Falls.

At the time of my last hike, half of the footlog's railing was missing (hacked away by vandals). Any attempt to cross the creek *via*, or to view the falls *from* the footbridge was an extremely dangerous one.

Approximately 60' high, Little Creek dances over hundreds of small ledges. The falls fan from a 10' width at the top, to 20' at the base. Aquatic plants, such as brook lettuce and foamflower thrive at its base.

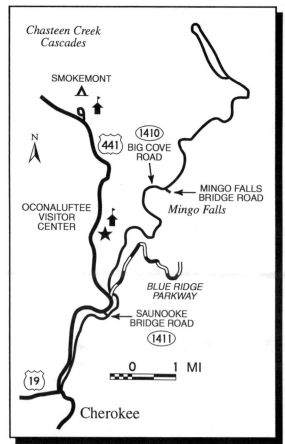

Chasteen Creek
Cascades

SMOKEMONT

N

441 1410
BIG COVE
ROAD

MINGO FALLS
BRIDGE ROAD

OCONALUFTEE
VISITOR
CENTER

Mingo Falls

BLUE RIDGE
PARKWAY

SAUNOOKE
BRIDGE ROAD
1411

0   1 MI

19

Cherokee

Chasteen Creek Cascade

Roads: Paved   A "2"
USGS Quadrangle:
Smokemont, NC
Bradley Fork & Chasteen
Creek trails, 1.95 miles,
moderate

Directions: From the Oconaluftee Visitor Center, take US 441 north for 3.4 miles to the Smokemont Campground turnoff. Turn right. After crossing a bridge spanning the Oconaluftee River, turn left. In .2 of a mile the road forks right, passes the ranger station, and forms a one-way loop through the campground. Year-round trail parking may be found at the Nature Trail parking area which is adjacent to campsite B-17 (approximately .5 of a mile from US 441). Seasonal parking, at the Bradley Fork Trailhead, is adjacent to campsite D-19.

From the Nature Trail parking area, hike north for just over .2 of a mile, through the "D" campground (the northernmost campground), to the gate and Bradley Fork Trailhead. After passing the trail signs the route turns steeply uphill, treading an old roadbed. While descending, at 710', the Hughes Ridge, Queen Mountain, and Toe String trails take off to the right. At the quarter mile pass an old pumphouse and soon thereafter a road that intersects from the right. From this point the trail undulates and meanders and at 1.1 miles crosses Chasteen Creek on a one-lane bridge. In just under 300' the road forks. The Chasteen Creek Trail begins here and treads the right fork, while the Bradley Fork Trail continues straight. (Signs give directions and distances.)

Hiking the Chasteen Creek Trail, in just over .1 of a mile pass campsite #50 which is barely visible on the right, through dense woods. Soon thereafter, cross Chasteen Creek on a one-lane footbridge. The trail is now very stony and

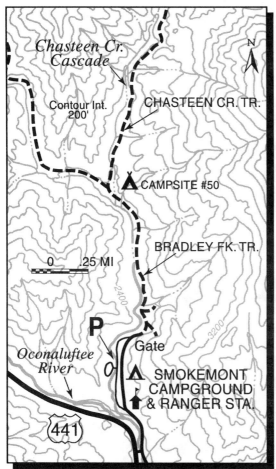

ascends at a moderate rate. For the most part, along this stretch, Chasteen Creek is unseen on account of thick rhododendron. At 1.85 miles look for the fall's side trail, which splits to the left and runs level, while the main trail continues right and ascends.

On the fall's side trail, in 100' pass a hitching post. The trail soon narrows to follow Chasteen Creek upstream. After having hiked 1.95 miles arrive at the cascade's viewing area.

With a total height of 15', Chasteen Creek runs in a cascade of 40'. Foaming white and sliding, its width is 12 to 15' at the top, fanning out to 40' at the base.

Hemlock, maple, mountain laurel, mountain magnolia, rhododendron, and yellow birch populate its environs. Ferns, Fraser's sedge, and partridgeberry crowd the forest floor.

Mingo Falls

Roads: Paved   An "8"   No hiking map needed.
USGS Quadrangle: Smokemont, NC
Mingo Falls Trail, .15 of a mile, difficult, on account of initial steepness

Directions: From the Great Smoky Mountains Oconaluftee Visitor Center, drive south on US 441 for 1.2 miles and turn left onto Saunooke Bridge Road (SR 1411). In .2 of a mile, after crossing the Oconaluftee River, intersect Big Cove Road (SR 1410) at a stop sign. Turn left (north) and reset the odometer. Travel 4.7 miles and turn right onto Mingo Falls Bridge Road. Cross the river. The parking area is approximately 150' south of the bridge. The trail begins on the right side of the parking area at a concrete headwall.

With the tumbling Mingo Creek on the right, the trail ascends steeply (on more than 150 steps) for 395′ and levels. The trail then undulates in the steep-sided ravine and at 770′ bends left to round a rock outcrop. Soon thereafter, cross the footbridge and arrive at the fall's viewing area.

This beautiful waterfall is more than 150′ high, with cascades below. Its bright, white waters photograph best when fully lit by the noonday sun. The diffused light of an overcast day also works well.

Rainbow Falls, GSMNP

Nantahala National Forest

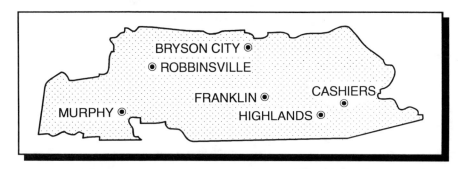

The Nantahala National Forest is North Carolina's largest with over one-half million acres. Cherokee, for land of the noonday sun, the name "Nantahala" was given to the river and its gorge which only taste light when the sun is high overhead. In this region you'll find waterfalls that require only the effort of driving, such as Cullasaja and Bridal Veil Falls. At the other end of the spectrum are their more difficult to reach counterparts, Sassafras Falls and the Lower Falls on Slickrock Creek. This area is home to the graceful and the mighty. Whitewater Falls, at 411', is thought to be the highest waterfall in the eastern US. In winter, when the creeks and rivers are running at their highest levels, one can hear the constant roar of Whitewater Falls almost one-half mile away.

I especially enjoyed the Nantahala's Snowbird Area. In the fall, the drive along FS 75 blazes in the orange of spotted touch-me-nots. Along the many streamside trails you may encounter the somewhat rare cardinal flower, whose chief pollinator is the hummingbird. You'll hear, but rarely see, the pileated woodpecker whose receding, jungle-like, cuk-cuk-cuk-cuk-cuk call announces its presence.

At many of the forest's falls you'll notice potholed rock. These holes are caused by stones being trapped in one spot by larger stones, then being jackhammered in place by the water's actions.

Murphy Area

Leatherwood Falls Loop Trail, Clay County, NC

Roads: Graveled   A "1"
USGS Quadrangle: Hayesville, NC
Trail #73, .7 of a mile, moderate

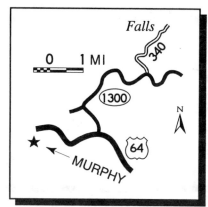

Directions: Where US 64 splits from US Hwys. 19/129/74, just east of Murphy, drive east on US 64 for 9.6 miles to Fires Creek Road (SR 1300, sign: Fires Creek Recreation Area). Turn left (north) and in .9 of a mile cross the Hiwassee River bridge. Drive a total of 3.95 miles to the graveled SR 1344 (Fires Creek Wildlife Road, shown on the map of the Nantahala National Forest as FS 340), which is on the left (sign: Fires Creek Recreation Area, 1.8 miles). In 1.9 miles cross Fires Creek on a bridge and immediately turn left into the parking area.

The loop trail doesn't offer a full view of the falls. However, they may be partially seen from the parking area by looking across Fires Creek and west up the Leatherwood Branch Cove (approximately 250' away). To see them fully, you'll have to wade the bone-chilling creek. When I visited this area in the dry season (fall), the creek was down and easily crossed, having only one deep spot. During my springtime visit, Fires Creek was far too swift and deep to be safely forded for a frontal view.

The trail begins on the right (east) side of the parking area at the information board. Initially the trail is paved.

From the parking area hike the paved trail and in 30' pass the information board. The trail makes a right then at 90' bends left to cross Fires Creek on an iron footbridge. Now on the north side of the creek, at 165' pass paths leading left and right to creekside picnic areas. At 215' arrive at the junction of the Cover Trail, which leads straight ahead. Continue left on the Leatherwood Loop Trail and at 415', after winding by several other secluded picnic spots, the paved trail ends with a sharp left turn (in the vicinity of the outhouse). The trail starts ascending. First heading north, the trail soon turns more westerly while passing through a hardwood forest on the steep mountain slope. Two tenths of a mile into the hike arrive at a boardwalk that skirts a boulder outcrop. To the left lie the cascades of Leatherwood Branch which precede the unseen falls that lay downstream. After viewing the cascades continue upstream.

The treadway now ascends over rock and roots alongside the cascading creek. Soon leveling while meandering through a laurel thicket, at .3 of a mile, amongst the white pines, cross Leatherwood Branch on a footbridge. In 80' arrive at the junction of the Rim Trail (#72). With a sharp left the Leatherwood Loop continues and once again joins Leatherwood Branch, on its west side. After passing several distant views of the aforementioned cascades, the trail descends slightly over a rocky and storm-damaged section, which is made narrow by the steep hillside. With a long right bend the treadway distances itself from the creek, then at .55 of a mile, in a descending left bend, heads back towards creek level. At just over .6 of a mile arrive back at the entry road. The route then turns left and crosses the concrete bridge (previously crossed) enroute to the parking area.

The falls best photograph under overcast conditions.

Snowbird - Tapoco Area

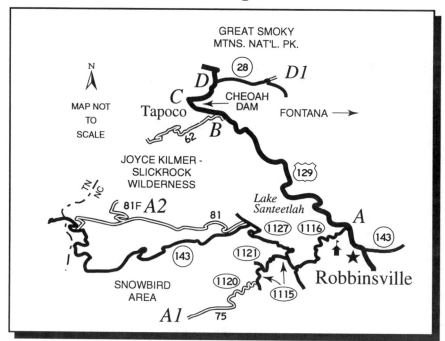

Both the Snowbird and the Joyce Kilmer-Slickrock Wilderness areas are in close proximity to the Smokies. As far as crowds go, however, they are many miles apart. The beautiful waterfalls of these wild areas rival any that I've seen—the solitude is like none found anywhere else.

Directions: From the intersection of US 129 and NC 143 in Robbinsville, drive north on US 129/NC 143 to the following points of interest. (Note: US 129 and NC 143 split at Massey Branch Road.)

A. Massey Branch Road (NC 143/SR 1116): 1.45 miles. Take NC 143/SR 1116 for 3.5 miles to access (1) the falls in the Snowbird Area, and (2) the falls in the Joyce Kilmer-Slickrock Wilderness Area.
B. Big Fat Gap Road (FS 62), access to Wildcat Falls via the Big Fat Trail: 14.15 miles. (Gated in winter. Contact Cheoah Ranger Station.)
C. Parking and trailhead for the Slickrock Creek Trail, access to Lower Falls: 15.9 miles.
D. The intersection of US 129 and NC 28 (near Deal's Gap): 18.1 miles. Take NC 28 the following distance to:
   D1. The Great Smoky Mountains National Park, Twentymile access (access to the Twentymile Cascades[1]): 2.9 miles.

[1] Though located in the Smokies, this waterfall is listed here because of its close proximity to the waterfalls in the Nantahala N. F.

A1. Snowbird Area, Graham County, NC

Roads: Graveled
USGS Quadrangle: Santeetlah Creek, NC
Trails: 64, 64A, & 65, 3.6 miles minimum, water crossings, moderate

This area was one of North Carolina's last to be settled by white men. In the 1830's settlements were established in the area north of Mouse Knob. In 1838 many Cherokee took refuge in the area's remoteness, while others were banished to Oklahoma on the infamous, "Trail of Tears." Some of their descendants still reside in the area. In 1908, a 1600 acre game reserve was established by a Mr. George Moore. Wealthy hunters paid to bag exotic animals brought in from both the western states and from abroad. The venture failed when many of the animals were poached or escaped. In the 1920's the Bemis Hardwood Lumber Company bought lands in the region for its virgin timbers. By 1942 over 100 million board feet of lumber had been hauled out by rail. The Snowbird Area was purchased by the Forest Service in 1943 and the land has made an astonishing comeback.

Today, some of the area's trails follow the railroad beds which fed the Buffalo-Snowbird Railroad. Many trails still have crossties in place. Trestles spanned many of the creeks, hollows, and ravines. Enroute to Sassafras Falls the trail makes several dips where the hollows were spanned by these trestles.

There are four waterfalls on the Snowbird Area trail map. Visiting all four in a day's time should be attempted by only the most seasoned hiker. The minimum hiking distance (to either Sassafras or Big Falls) is 3.6 miles one-way.

Directions: The Snowbird Area is reached from the intersection of Massey Branch Road (NC 143/SR 1116) and Snowbird Road (NC 143/SR 1127) by

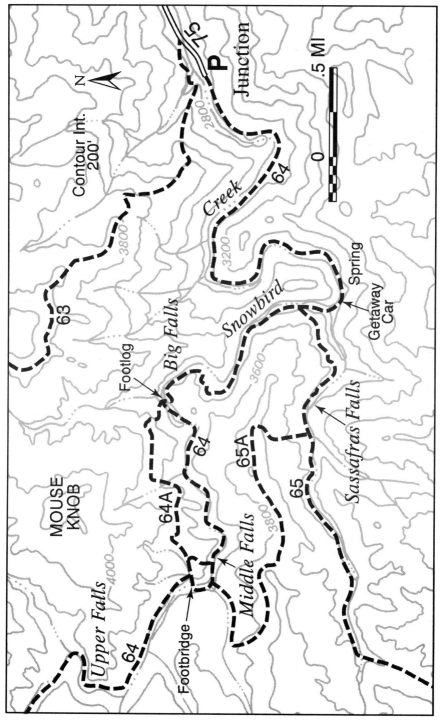

driving north on NC 143/SR 1127 for 2.1 miles. Turn left (west) onto SR 1115 (also called Snowbird Road) and in 2.1 miles arrive at a three-way intersection. (At this location SR 1115 bends sharply left, retaining its route number, after being intersected from the right by SR 1121.) Turn sharply left and continue 1 additional mile. After crossing Snowbird Creek on a concrete bridge, turn right onto SR 1120, which upon entering the Nantahala National Forest changes to FS 75. Drive 6.15 miles to its end, at Junction, which at one time was the railhead for the Buffalo-Snowbird Railroad. The trail, if not marked, is 50' to the left of the information board (the southernmost trail).

Big Snowbird Trail (#64): As you enter the woods this blue-blazed trail passes over numerous jeep-blocking mounds. Soon, it becomes more conducive to hiking—gently ascending alongside Snowbird Creek. In .7 and again at .8 of a mile cross small creeks. At 1.5 miles pass a jeep-blocking boulder. Continuing its ascent, at mile 2.3 the trail levels as you approach a piped spring. Two and one-half miles into the hike, arrive at an open area with a confusing "Y" intersection. Disregard the path on the left. Take the trail to the right (north) and in 30' notice the "getaway car" parked for eternity under a hemlock. The trail makes an "S" here and descends slightly to cross Sassafras Creek on steppingstones. Upon reaching the creek's north side, pass a primitive campsite lying to the right. The Big Snowbird Trail once again ascends, now on an east-facing slope. Trillium blooms early in this warmer microclimate. At just over 2.8 miles arrive at the silver-blazed Sassafras Creek Trail (#65) which intersects from the left.

Sassafras Creek Trail (#65): To visit Sassafras Falls, hike the Sassafras Creek Trail and in .8 of a mile reach a point where they're heard from the trail (they're also visible when the leaves are off). Look for a slim, descending path which leads 250' through waist-high growth and over rubble to the base area.

This pristine treasure of the woods features rock that is pockmarked with potholes. The rock face splits the creek into three streams and the majority of its waters flow over the right side. Of the four waterfalls I've seen in the area, this is my favorite. It also seems to be the least visited. Return to the Big Snowbird Trail and continue upstream.

Big Falls: Continuing up the Big Snowbird Trail, now at a moderate rate, there is an abundance of in-the-trail crossties. (It seems that mineral-laden water from wet-weather branches acts to preserve them.) The trail crosses several wet-weather branches, one of special note, at 3.25 miles, has created a wash that affords fine views of Snowbird Creek and a small, midstream island far below. Losing sight and sound of the creek, in a long right bend, the trail outlines two hollows, much like an "M." In their depths the treadway undulates over rock and roots and for the moment becomes more difficult. Exiting the hollows with a left bend, at 3.6 miles the trail straightens and becomes easier. In approximately 300' look carefully for the steep access to the lower portion of Big Falls. Scramble down the slope and in 150' reach the base of Big Falls.

Big Falls is a 400'-long series of cascades over a wide rock expanse with scoured-out swirlholes. Looking upstream the scene is one of cascade after cascade, with a small waterfall topping them off.

To reach the upper portion of the cascades, return to the main trail and hike upstream approximately 450' to a barely-discernible side path leading to creek level. (Preceding this path, look for a large [100' long], noticeable boulder outcrop, on the left, where the railroad bed was blasted into the side of the mountain.) The side path descends steeply for 80' through a tunnel of rhododendron to the creek bank. Once there, you must lower yourself to the bedrock viewing area of the upper tier.

The upper portion of this waterfall falls in 3' steps then makes a 10' slide over smooth bedrock into a bottomless pool. The outstanding feature here is the beautiful rock. In early spring the starlike, white flowers of serviceberry are among the first to be seen streamside. As well, its red-green leaves add color to the gray, woodland backdrop.

Middle Falls: Back on the main trail, continue upstream. At 3.8 miles arrive at a confusing split. The correct route veers left and ascends the sloping crest of a ridge, treading in-ground steps, while the old railroad bed continues straight ahead. Descending the far side of the ridge, the trail then switchbacks down to cross Snowbird Creek on a footlog-type footbridge. Now on the north side of the creek, pass through a primitive campsite and in 110' (from the bridge, 3.9 miles into the hike) intersect the Middle Falls Trail.

The Forest Service is encouraging use of the Middle Falls Trail to access Middle and Upper Falls, instead of the old route (the Big Snowbird Trail), as it is less dangerous. I prefer this route, as well, as it allows year-round access.

Middle Falls Trail (#64A): The Middle Falls Trail climbs steeply, in ramp fashion, then switchbacks to gain a total of 280' in elevation ascending Mouse Knob. Now on higher ground, the trail undulates and meanders westerly. At 4.2 miles top a saddle and descend into the hollow of a small, unnamed creek. In .2 of a mile the trail turns sharply left as it nears this bubbling creek. Hiking downstream, in 60' cross the creek on the remains of a logging bridge. In another 65' the trail turns sharply right and treads a rutted logging road (for a short distance). After ascending moderately, the trail levels off and undulates on the south slopes of Mouse Knob. Four and three-fourths miles into the hike, atop a ridge, the trail turns abruptly right, then in 125' turns sharply left and descends the low point of a hollow. At 4.85 miles cross to the left side of a small, boggy branch that rises in this hollow. At this crossing there are the remains of an old logging bridge, as well. At 4.95 miles arrive at the Middle Falls Side Trail. (A sign called attention to this intersection at the time of my hike.)

Middle Falls Side Trail: Hike the Middle Falls Side Trail and in 830' arrive at the blue-blazed Big Snowbird Trail. Hike downstream for 335' and arrive at the side path to Middle Falls. Take the side path for 180' to the base area.

The fall's rock face is over 100' wide with the creek occupying half of its width. The bedrock is uniformly curved at the top, and the falls splash in a cascade of 15' into a large and very deep pool.

To reach Upper Falls return to the Middle Falls Trail.

Upper Falls: Continuing towards Upper Falls, the orange-blazed Middle Falls Trail bends sharply right and descends to cross a creek in approximately 100'. The trail then ascends and tops a point of land and descends once again. At just over 5 miles, the Middle Falls Trail intersects the blue-blazed Big Snowbird Trail which continues both north and south. Northbound, the trail heads towards a creek, approximately 50' away. Southbound (left) it crosses Snowbird Creek on a suspension-type footbridge, approximately 40' away.

Hiking north, towards Upper Falls, the trail dips and immediately crosses the aforementioned tributary of Snowbird Creek, then undulates while heading upstream along the east bank of Snowbird Creek. In approximately 700', the trail dips and crosses a small, wet-weather branch then treads the old logging railroad bed once again. After treading through several wet spots and passing several fire rings, while heading northwesterly, at 5.75 miles the trail makes a gradual bend north, in harmony with the creek. At 5.8 miles make an abrupt right where the logging railroad once crossed the creek on a trestle. The trail now narrows and becomes more difficult as it undulates upstream along a rocky and root-laced slope, deeply shaded by dense rhododendron. (This slope has a few treacherous spots, with steep, creekside drop-offs and jagged rock.) In .15 of a mile (5.95 miles) arrive in the vicinity of the base of Upper Falls. The trail is in the creek's flood plain here and after heavy rainfall may be under water.

Upper Falls is a shoaling waterfall, approximately 100' in length and 15' high. There is no safe frontal view, as the pool is too deep. A side view of this waterfall lies 210' upstream.

To reach this viewpoint, hike uphill through the rhododendron thicket and reintersect the old logging railroad bed alongside the falls.

Joyce Kilmer - Slickrock Wilderness Area

A2. Falls on Cold Branch, Graham County, NC

Roads: High Clearance   A "3" 30'
USGS Quadrangle: Santeetlah Creek, NC
No official trail, 200', easy, (no hiking map needed)

Note: FS 81 may be gated. Before committing to this long drive check with the Cheoah Ranger Station, located on Massey Branch Road. FS 81F is one lane and very steep. After viewing the falls, drive up the mountain .3 of a mile further and use the pullout on the left as a turnaround.

Directions: From the intersection of Massey Branch Road (NC 143/SR 1116) and NC 143/SR 1127, drive north on 143/1127 (Snowbird Road, soon changing to Santeetlah Road) for 7 miles to a double left turn at Santeetlah Gap. The first left is the Cherohala Skyway (NC 143 West), the second left is FS 81 (a descending paved road that soon gives way to gravel) the route to the falls. FS 81 descends into the Santeetlah Creek drainage and in 1.4 miles crosses a concrete bridge. At 3.5 miles arrive at the Stewart Cabin. (Stop for a local history lesson.) Drive a total of 6.8 miles to FS 81F. Turn right onto FS 81F and drive .3 of a mile to the pullout on the left side of the road. Be very careful here. The road is narrow with just enough room for parking and another car to pass. Look to the left for the barely visible falls which are approximately 200' off the road.

Negotiate your way down the bank and wade through the waist-high growth. Look for a hole in the laurel to gain access to the creek.

This waterfall is broader than it is high. Its rock face is laced with potholes. What really caught my eye, though, was the cove downstream, whose boulders are covered in the greenest of mosses.

Slickrock Creek Area

To hike from Big Fat Gap and visit both Wildcat and Lower Falls then exit at Cheoah Dam (Tapoco) requires a 10 mile hike with 12 stream crossings. You'll experience backcountry that few others see. This venture requires an overnight stay. I had the pleasure of having my brother with me. Both of us were in awe of the beauty we beheld. This is my most memorable outdoor experience. Good company all around.

Since the Slickrock Creek Trail is not blazed and few people venture into its more remote areas, the little-worn track often leaves you scratching your head and wondering ??? which way to go.

There are 3 major stream crossings between Big Fat Gap and Wildcat Falls, and only 1, if hiking in from Tapoco to Lower Falls. Connecting all the way through (as mentioned above) requires 8 additional fords of varying difficulty. We had the good fortune of finding crossings that were no more than knee-deep. Portions of the streambed were dry. However, from all the woodland debris snagged in trees and deposited in the *then* dry portion of the streambed, we knew the creek could be a dangerous, raging torrent in full flow. If you were to get snowed or iced in here, your stay would be a lengthy one. Any route out would be treacherous on account of the rock exposures. Between Tapoco and the Slickrock Creek drainage, boardwalks skirt what would otherwise be impassable rock outcrops.

Along the Slickrock Creek Trail we found all sorts of artifacts from the days of logging by rail: brake shoes; brake cylinders; cables; crossties with spikes; rail; and a knuckle.

B. Wildcat Falls, Graham Co., NC, Monroe Co., TN

Roads: Graveled,   A "10" 3 tiers of equal height (10')
Map: Joyce Kilmer-Slickrock Wilderness, Trails: #41 (Big Fat Trail),
#44 (Nichols Cove Trail), #42 (Slickrock Creek Trail)
2.75 miles, potentially deep water crossings, difficult

Note: As stated above, this route connects with Lower Falls then eventually ends at Tapoco. Visiting both requires an overnight stay and a grand total of 12 creek crossings.

Directions: From US 129 take FS 62 (Big Fat Gap Road) for 7.2 miles to the parking area at Big Fat Gap.

The trail enters the woods on the west side of the parking area (behind the information board) and descends steeply into a flower-filled hollow. Every variety of trillium imaginable thrives on the moist slopes.

Winding while descending, the trail encounters a wet-weather branch at .35 of a mile where it turns sharply left. At .45 of a mile the trail crosses a rocky, wet spot. (This, and other soon to be encountered trickles, are the headwaters of Big Fat Branch, which will accompany us for a mile, or so.) At .55 of a mile cross to the north side of the wet-weather branch. The trail then turns sharply left and continues to descend along its north side. At just over .75 of a mile pass a confusing path (the old trail) leading straight ahead. With a left turn the trail dips to cross to the south side of what has become Big Fat Branch. The trail now treads an old, but well-defined roadbed and for the next half mile descends at a lesser rate, and crosses several wet-weather branches.

At 1.25 miles the route turns sharply right and switchbacks into the creek bottom. Often within sight of the creek, the trail now more closely follows Big Fat Branch downstream. At 1.6 miles arrive at the intersection of the Nichols Cove Trail (#44). Veer left here. At 1.65 miles intersect the Slickrock Creek Trail (#42) which leads both left and right. Veer right, and in 200', after passing through a primitive campsite, arrive at beautiful Slickrock Creek. The trail crosses to the creek's west side here, to tread an old logging railroad bed. (Trail location may be tough here, as hikers have taken different routes to cross the creek. On my visits I found a suitable crossing 200' upstream from this prominent campsite.)

Upon crossing Slickrock Creek, immediately tread a rock outcrop and pass

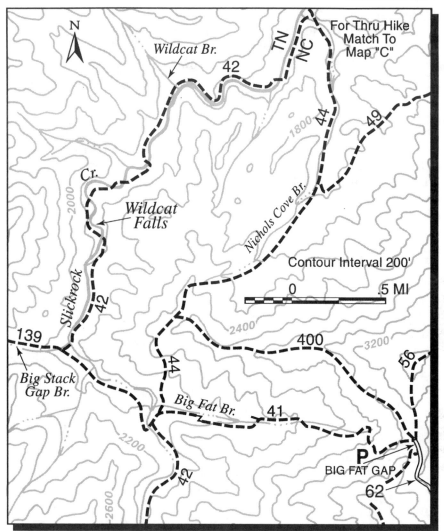

through an open hardwood forest. Just downstream, the railroad bed is built up, out of the creek's flood plain. At 2.05 miles the trail bends slightly left, away from Slickrock Creek, and soon crosses a wet-weather branch. Treading closer to the creek, at just over 2.1 miles, pass over a very narrow and slick, rock outcrop which is constricted by shale cliffs, on the left, and the creek, on the right. Just shy of 2.2 miles the trail dips to cross an unnamed creek. At 2.35 miles, in the vicinity of Big Stack Gap Branch, arrive at the intersection of the Big Stack Gap Branch Trail (#139). Approximately 50′downstream from this intersection cross to the east (North Carolina) side of Slickrock Creek. Two and sixty-five hundredths miles into the hike, pass to the right of a prominent fire ring. In 80′the trail dips to cross to the Tennessee side of Slickrock Creek.

Upon crossing, the trail bends left while rounding a slick and tricky, rock outcrop. The falls lie to the right of this outcrop. Passing alongside them, the treadway widens while descending to a full view of Wildcat Falls.

This is a very beautiful, triple waterfall flowing in an "S" bend in the creek. The upper tier is distant while the lower and middle tiers are more closely stationed. The middle tier has dimpled and potholed bedrock with crisscrossing veins of quartz. The lower tier splashes into a large, blue-green pool brimming with hundreds of colorful, rounded stones. A small, rocky, driftwood-strewn island, of sorts, lies downstream. Birch and alder thrive here.

Flowers seen in the springtime, on this hike, include: at least 6 varieties of trillium, rue anemone, Mayapple, bloodroot, geraniums, jack-in-the-pulpit, smooth Solomon's seal, and foamflower.

C. Lower Falls on Slickrock Creek, Graham Co., NC, Monroe Co., TN

Roads: Paved,　A　"4"　10'
Map: Joyce Kilmer-Slickrock Wilderness
Trail #42, 3.1 miles, water crossing, difficult

Note: This trail goes on to connect with Wildcat Falls (see above).

This is a rugged hike over undulating and very rocky terrain. The trail looks deceptively easy on the official hiking map.

Directions: Just before the US 129 Bridge over Calderwood Lake (near the Cheoah Dam, at Tapoco) look for a slim, graveled road on the left. This leads to trail parking near a sewage treatment plant .1 of a mile ahead. The official trailhead and information board lie 200' ahead (north).

At the outset, this hike is a pleasant, near shoreline trek alongside Calderwood Lake. The steep mountainsides are a veritable flower garden, sporting a succession of trillium, foamflower, and fringed phacelia. In .5 of a mile the treadway narrows to a single track. Six-tenths of a mile into the hike, after a slight ascent, arrive at the Ike Branch Trail (#45) which splits leading west. Continuing, at .7 of a mile, the trail outlines the Ike Branch Cove and crosses its creek on a footbridge. As you exit the cove, the lake comes back into view. At .9 of a mile, round a rock outcrop that is girdled by a rickety boardwalk. You'll encounter three more of these structures on this rugged stretch of trail, all of them in an advanced state of decline.

One and six-tenths miles into the hike, reach a high point with a becoming view of Calderwood Lake to the northwest. The trail bends 90° left here and crosses the wilderness boundary while entering Slickrock Creek's Cove. Soon descending, at 1.75 miles pass a steep pathway that leads down to Calderwood Lake. After traversing some storm damage, at 1.9 miles reach the creek bottom and pass a path that leads downstream to the lake, as well. Just ahead, tread a slick

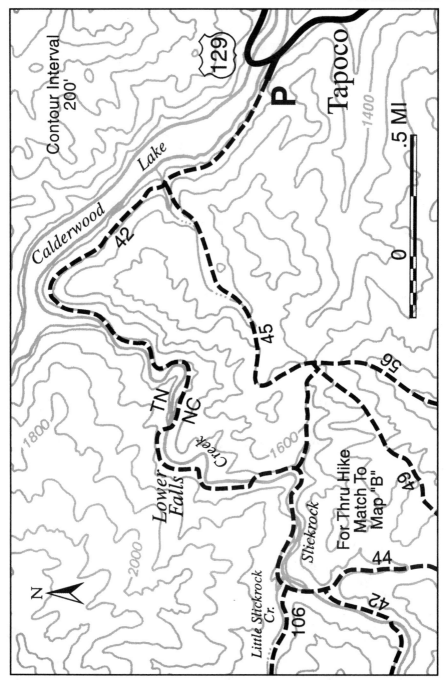

and jagged rock outcrop in the creek's overflow area. High water would narrow the trail significantly here. Soon thereafter, several primitive campsites are encountered. Two and one-tenth miles into the hike reach a potentially confusing area. Here, a slim path leads to the creek, while the trail goes left and uphill to circumvent the impassable, boulder-filled creek. At 2.2 miles, in a right bend, notice the 150'-high rock wall on the left. At 2.45 miles arrive at a very tricky, rock outcrop. Consisting of slate, the treadway is very narrow, it's also slick, and angles towards the creek, which is fairly deep. Water seeping from this rock would make this stretch impassable in freezing weather. During periods of high water the approach to this outcrop may be under water. Be especially careful with a packframe as you make an off-balance pass to avoid hanging on the rock. There is a slim, high-water route to the left of this ledge, however.

Just ahead lies a beautiful, rocky area which makes for tough going. During the rainy season the trail would be in the creek here. Cross a small, unnamed creek as the route becomes more woodland oriented. At 2.75 miles the trail is forced to the Tennessee side of Slickrock Creek by an impassable rock outcrop. After a knee-deep crossing, continue upstream soon treading the old railroad grade. At 3 miles, dip to cross a small, cascading tributary with a 6 to 8' waterfall to the trail's right. In another .1 of a mile arrive at Lower Falls.

Slickrock Creek makes a flat run towards the viewer then spills in split-flow fashion for 15' into a large, blue-green pool. A tree dotted island of rounded rock bounds the pool. Look for a bent piece of rail on this island. Although the falls are not large, their surroundings make them very beautiful.

D. The intersection of US 129 and NC 28 at Deal's Gap (as above).

D1. Twentymile Cascades, Great Smoky Mtns. NP, Swain County, NC[1]

Roads: Graveled   A "3"
USGS Quadrangles: Tapoco, NC, TN, Fontana Dam, NC, in their margins
Twentymile Creek Trail, .65 of a mile, easy

Directions: From the intersection of US 129 and NC 28 (Deal's Gap), take NC 28 for 2.9 miles to the Great Smoky Mountains National Park, Twentymile entrance. Drive the graveled access road for .15 of a mile, passing the ranger station, enroute to the parking area which is on the right.

From the parking area, hike the graveled road north and in 145' arrive at the gate. The road that serves as the trail initially ascends at an easy rate while heading northeast. To the right, approximately 60 to 70' away, Twentymile Creek rushes over rock. With a gradual bend, the road heads east. At the quarter-mile look for a slim path leading to a creekside clearing. In spring, this open spot is filled with wildflowers. At one third of a mile the roadbed bends noticeably left to head northeast once again. At .5 of a mile pass a disused

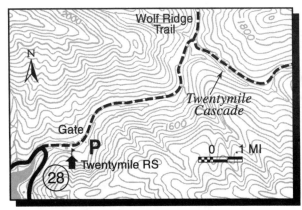

parking area on the left. Fifty-five hundredths of a mile into the hike, cross Moore Springs Branch on a wooden bridge, just above its confluence with Twentymile Creek. In 50' the Wolf Ridge Trail originates to the left, while the Twentymile Creek Trail (to the cascade) leads right.

Ascend the graveled road. After bending slightly left the road straightens to head in a more easterly direction. Six tenths of a mile into the hike look for a side trail with a marker stating, "Twentymile Cascades." This side trail leads off in a "Y" fashion and treads level, at first, then descends to a side view of the cascade. Alongside the cascade the trail bends right and leads downstream to the base viewing area.

The cascade is approximately 15' high (total) and runs for 80 to 90'. Ten feet wide at the top, it fans out to a width of 40 to 50' at the base. First cascading over bedrock, then through boulders, the last 7' (in height) is a 45° slide over a bedrock exposure. Its waters make a bubbly slip into a small pool. The creek exits the right side of the pool area. When viewed from the base, much of the fall is obscured by dense laurel and rhododendron.

[1] This waterfall is listed here because of its close proximity to the waterfalls in the Nantahala N. F.

Topton Area

Falls in the Nantahala Gorge, Macon County, NC

Roads: Paved   A "4" & A "4" respectively
USGS Quadrangles: Topton, Hewitt, NC
Seen from car or short path

Directions: From the intersection of US Hwys. 19/74 and 129, in the community of Topton, drive north on US 19/74 for 2.1 miles to the community of Beechertown. Turn right (east) onto Wayah Road (SR 1412/ 1310, sign: Nantahala River Launch Site) and drive up the Nantahala River Gorge. In approximately 3.7 miles, arrive at the first of two pullouts with beautiful overlooks of the cascading Nantahala River. Drive a total of 4.3 miles to a pullout, on the right, for Whiteoak Falls.

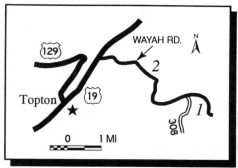

1. Whiteoak Falls

Seen from the shoulder of the road, this waterfall cascades over a jagged rock face. Mustard-colored lichens adorn a rock wall on the far side of the creek. Notice how the creekbed has been worn smooth by the water's abrasiveness.

A distant, frontal view can be had from Old River Road (FS 308). To reach this viewpoint, drive .1 of a mile downstream, turn left, cross the bridge spanning Whiteoak Creek, and park on its south side. A slim, boulder-strewn path leads up the north side of the creek to the base area.

Being next to Wayah Road, Whiteoak Falls is a target for litterbugs. I hauled out a whole sack full of trash and barely made a dent in all of it. It also seems that litter from upstream sources snags on its jagged rocks. It is still a beautiful place and well worth visiting. Please do so with a litter bag in hand.

2. Falls on Camp Branch

Seen from two pullouts on the right (east) side of Wayah Road, 1.5 miles *downstream* from Whiteoak Falls. The first pullout offers a view of the upper tier. The lower tier is seen from the second pullout 300' ahead. There is no access to the base, as the falls lie across the Nantahala River.

Camp Branch falls between steep, V-shaped mountainsides as a series of cascades. Winter offers the best views, as the upper tier may be hidden by vegetation in the warm months. The lower tier can be seen year-round. When the sun hits just right, its waters totally whiteout. Camp Branch makes a cascading entry into the Nantahala River.

Franklin Area

This is North Carolina's gemstone region. Garnet, rubies, and corundum are mined here. Many area creeks show color in their sands.

The locations listed below reside in Macon County, unless otherwise noted.

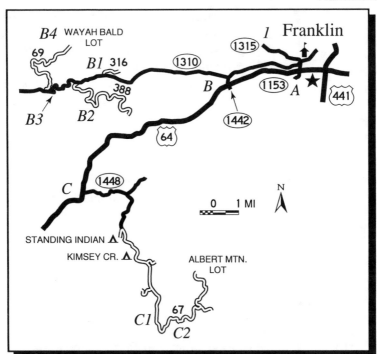

Directions: From the intersection of US Hwys. 441 and 64, in Franklin, drive west on US 64 to access the following points of interest:

A. Sloan Road (SR 1153), access to the Falls on Wallace Branch: 1 mile.

B. SR 1442, access to the Falls on Camp Branch, Rough Fork Falls, Berties Falls, and the Wayah Bald Observation Tower: 3.9 miles.

C. West Old Murphy Road (SR 1448, Old US 64), access to the Falls in the Southern Nantahala Wilderness: 12.2 miles.

A. Falls on Wallace Branch

Roads: Paved   A "1" total height 20', with a run of approximately 35 to 40'
USGS Quadrangle: Franklin, NC
Bartram Trail, yellow blaze, .15 of a mile, easy

A. Directions: Turn right onto Sloan Road (SR 1153, pass the US Forest Service, Wayah Ranger Station) and in .3 of a mile intersect Old Murphy Road (SR 1442) at a stop sign. (The route now makes a slight jog.) Turn left and immediately (in 50') make a right onto Pressley Road (SR 1315). Reset your odometer and travel this paved road for 1.75 miles to the Bartram Trail (graveled) parking area. (To assure that you're in the correct location, look for a gated road that forks left at the end of the pavement, while the parking area forks right.) A sign at the trailhead states, "Wallace Branch, Bartram Trail."

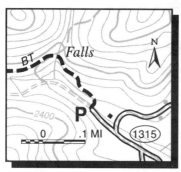

The Bartram Trail enters the woods on the right (north) side of the parking area and immediately crosses Wallace Branch on a footbridge. Leading uphill at a moderate rate for the first 390', the trail then levels slightly. Descending at an easy rate from this point, at 690' arrive at a second footbridge and the base of the falls.

The falls are of the sliding variety and should be seen after adequate rainfall. The best time to visit is in the spring, as there is more water and streamside vegetation. Plants and trees to be seen trailside and around the falls, include: ferns, hearts-a-bustin, Indian pipe, several varieties of trillium, jack-in-the-pulpit, foamflower, and alder.

B. Directions: At this location turn right (north) onto SR 1442 (Old Murphy Road, across the highway from Mt. Hope Baptist Church). In approximately .2 of a mile turn left onto SR 1310 (Wayah Road). Drive the following distances to the points of interest listed below:

B1. FS 316, access to the Falls on Camp Branch: 5.3 miles.

B2. FS 388, access to Rough Fork Falls: 6.55 miles.

B3. Berties Falls: 8.9 miles.

B4. FS 69, access to the Wayah Bald Observation Tower: 9.2 miles.

B1. Falls on Camp Branch

Roads: Graveled   Lower A "3" 8', Upper A "2" 12'
USGS Quadrangle: Wayah Bald, NC
Woodland pathway, .25 of a mile, minor water crossing, easy-moderate

Directions: From Wayah Road, take FS 316 for .15 of a mile to the parking area at the fork. This hike begins at the gate 75' north of the parking area. *Do not take the road that crosses the bridge at this location.*

From the gate, the old roadbed serving as our treadway ascends at an easy to moderate rate within earshot of the rushing Camp Branch. Brief glimpses of the creek, to the right side of the pathway, are quite beautiful. At .15 of a mile pass to the left of an 8 by 12' concrete building. (The old roadbed that serves as the pathway is wide and clear up to this point, then narrows significantly.) In 170' pass a smaller (4 by 6') concrete block building, on the left, off the path some 15 to 20'. Just ahead, the pathway dips to cross a small branch. The treadway's ascent now steepens. At .2 of a mile look for a slim path heading towards the creek that leaves the main path at a 45° angle. Take this side path and in 70' arrive at a small pool and the lower fall's viewing area.

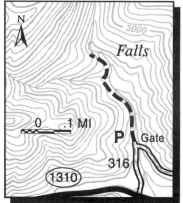

This is a pretty waterfall, although it is small (only 8' high). It spills as a broken fall of 3' which then shoots off the bedrock, splashing into a 15 by 20' pool. The pool is rather deep, with hundreds of smooth stones. The bedrock face is approximately 40' wide and shows its grain very beautifully. A swirl-hole on its right side fills with water when the creek is running high. The rock exposure's right side is covered in light green to gray lichens.

Return to the main pathway and hike upstream. In 220' arrive at a side view of the sliding, upper falls. Backtrack 30' from the side view and look for a safe route to the base (reached by scrambling down through the rhododendron preceding the fall's rock exposure). (The route I took is between a prominent rock outcrop and a large chestnut stump.)

The upper falls slide at a 40° angle over a bedrock exposure that is approximately 25' wide. The creek flows for 6' down the middle of the exposure as a 3'-wide flume of white water. It is then split in half to flow the remaining 6' down the middle and right sides of the exposure. The upper falls are housed in a U-shaped, cirque-like opening, surrounded by rhododendron, some hemlock, and a scattering of maple. Where not moss covered, the brown rock glistens.

Because of harsh lighting, the falls are best photographed on an overcast day, or in the early morning, or late afternoon when the sun is hidden behind the ridge.

B2. Rough Fork Falls, Rufus Morgan Trail

Roads: Graveled   A "5" 60'
USGS Quadrangle: Wayah Bald, NC
Trail #27, .5 of a mile, water crossings, moderate-difficult

Directions: At this location turn left (south) onto FS 388, pass through the gate and drive 2.1 miles to the A. Rufus Morgan parking area and trailhead. Park here. The fall's trail is on the north side of the Left Prong of Rough Fork Creek. (Don't be confused by a creekside road, 100' south of the parking area, as it does not lead to the falls.)

The trail enters the woods and immediately bends right. Initially ascending rather steeply, in switchback fashion, at 440' the trail levels somewhat, and in a long right bend enters the hollow of a small branch. At .25 of a mile cross this branch. In early spring, look for large-flowered bellwort and showy orchis in this area. The trail once again ascends and in 135' crosses an old roadbed.

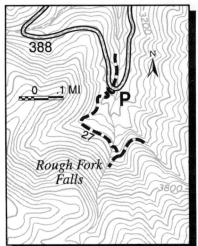

388

Rough Fork
Falls

After topping a small rise, at .4 of a mile, the trail descends slightly and in 100' crosses the fall's branch, where it immediately turns upstream. Just ahead lies a 10' sliding waterfall. At its base the trail turns sharply left and continues ascending. The upper falls become visible in this area. To obtain a better view, continue upstream. At .45 of a mile the trail makes a sharp right while a confusing path leads straight ahead. Ascend the fall's cove and at just over one-half mile arrive at the base area.

This 60' waterfall shoots out of the rhododendron and over the edge, foaming white as it tumbles down the rock face. Multitudes of trillium and white violets crowd its left slope.

B3. Berties Falls

Seen from paved road   A "1"
USGS Quadrangle: Wayah Bald, NC

Note: Please visit this waterfall after heavy rainfall and during the growing season for best viewing.

At this location look for the graveled pullout on the right (north) side of the road. Park here. Walk the road east for 100' to the fall's roadside viewing area.

Seen on the south side of Wayah Road, this is a broken cascade, with a total visible drop of 15 to 20'. Being high in the drainage, even after substantial rainfall there is little water. The hardwood-filled cove is very steep and rocky and has many moss-covered logs. There are more cascades to be seen higher up the mountainside (when the leaves are off). Passing under the road the branch eventually joins Wayah Creek.

Plants and trees seen here, include: foamflower, pale and spotted touch-me-nots, Mayapple, yellow birch and rhododendron.

B4. FS 69 (as above).

C. Directions: At this location, turn left (south) onto SR 1448 and drive 1.9 miles to FS 67, which is on the right (sign: "Standing Indian Campground"). Take FS 67 to these points of interest:

C1. Big Laurel Falls: 7 miles (pullout with sign).
C2. Mooney Falls: 7.65 miles (pullout with sign).

C1. Big Laurel Falls

Roads: Graveled   A "6" 20'
Map: Southern Nantahala Wilderness and Standing Indian Basin
Trail #29, .6 of a mile, no blaze, moderate

Note: The trail is initially blue blazed as its treadway is shared by the Timber Ridge Trail.

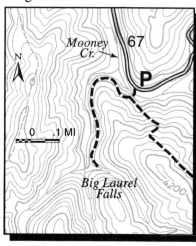

After the initial switchback-like descent, at 270' cross Mooney Creek on a footbridge. The Timber Ridge Trail immediately makes a sharp left and heads upstream, while the fall's trail bends right leading downstream. Entering the Big Laurel Creek drainage, at .15 of a mile, the trail bends left. At just over .2 of a mile the trail again bends left. In this vicinity, begin an undulating (moderate) ascent to the falls. At .6 of a mile arrive at the fall's viewing area.

Ease of access makes this a highly visited location.

C2. Mooney Falls

Roads: Graveled   A "4"
Trail #31, 5 minutes, moderate, (no hiking map needed)

The trail enters the woods and parallels the road for 290'. It then turns left and switchbacks to creek level. At the end of the first, and beginning of the second switchback (390') look for a side trail, on the left, leading 95' to the base of the upper tier.

Continuing, the main trail again switchbacks and at 720' arrives at the viewing area for the lower tier.

Mooney Falls is at its best with a clear-blue sky as a backdrop. Wintertime affords the best views. With higher water levels and the leaves being off, you're allowed a frontal view not available during other seasons.

Highlands Area

This area is divided into three routes with waterfalls along US 64, NC 106, and NC 28 South (see text).

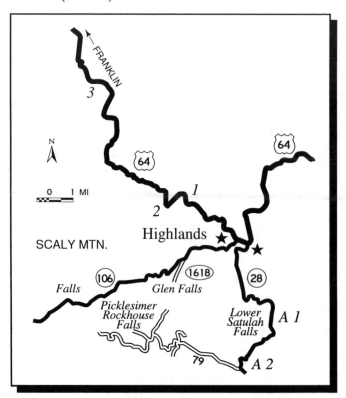

Via US 64

One of the region's most scenic and popular drives, the Mountain Waters National Scenic Byway (US 64) travels the length of the Cullasaja River Gorge, following the river's every turn. In June, flame azalea and laurels lend color to this waterfall drive. As well, autumn color comes early to this highland route. Eyes glued to this curvaceous road and good brakes are a safety must.

Directions: From the intersection of US 64 and NC 106, in Highlands, drive west on US 64 to the following points of interest. All are located on pavement and reside in Macon County.

1. Bridal Veil Falls: 2.35 miles.
2. FS 630 (the parking area for Dry Falls): 3.25 miles.
3. Cullasaja Falls: 8.9 miles.

1. Bridal Veil Falls

USGS Quadrangle: Highlands, NC   A "4"
Can be seen from car

A paved, semicircular pullout on the north side of US 64 leads behind the falls. Park, and while out of the car, step back to see its upper reaches. During the dry months this waterfall is a mere trickle.

Tufts of moss and lichen are seen growing on the flanks of its quartz-veined rock. Toadskin lichen (rock tripe) is abundant on the left. Laurels add their color in June. The upper tier clings to the rock face in a 30', foaming cascade. The falls then drop a sheer 40' into a culvert, which carries its waters under US 64.

2. Dry Falls

USGS Quadrangle: Highlands, NC   A "7" 40' No hiking map needed.
Easy, US Fee Area, Daily fee good for date of purchase at other FS sites.

A paved trail leads from the parking area for .2 of a mile to the base of the falls. Walk behind this powerful waterfall to a viewing area on its west side.

While visiting Dry Falls study the beautiful mosses and lichens on the overhanging rock. Clumps of aquatic plants and ferns grow in the rock's fissures.

I visited most recently after heavy rainfall. Water filled the river's entire course. The falls had an earth-shaking, almost deafening roar about them. So loud were they, that someone standing next to you couldn't be heard, unless they shouted at the top of their lungs. The Cullasaja leaped over the cliff, like water shot from a fire plug. Its waters, normally clear and bright white, were stained light brown with sediments. The *normal* dry pass behind them was a misty and drenching one.

3. Cullasaja Falls

USGS Quadrangle: Scaly Mountain, NC   A "7" 250'

Look for a paved pullout, on the left, providing the viewpoint for this waterfall. The pullout is located in a blind curve on one of the most dangerous stretches of US 64. Turning left (crossing traffic) into the pullout should not be attempted. As well, there is no room to turn around. To safely visit them, drive another mile, or so, turn around and return.

Cullasaja is a thundering giant, falling into a deep and rustic, rocky gorge. In summer, deciduous trees beautifully frame the falls and its gray cliffs that are adorned with yellow-green lichens. Several interestingly shaped trees top the right side of the falls, adding a mystical quality to them. Roadside litter detracts from this glorious place.

Easy access, high water levels, and the chance to view them under icy conditions, make winter a great time to visit all three of these locations.

Via NC 106

Glen Falls

Roads: Graveled   Upper A "6", Middle An "8", Lower A "2"
USGS Quadrangle: Highlands, NC
Trail #8, Overlook: moderate, Base and Lower: difficult

Directions: From the intersection of US 64 and NC 106, in Highlands, drive south on 106 for 1.8 miles. Turn left onto SR 1618 and in 1.1 miles arrive at the parking area and trailhead.

The trail enters the woods and in 425' arrives at an open spot with a limited view of the mountains to the south. The trail turns right, descends two switchbacks, and parallels the East Fork of Overflow Creek downstream. The first open view of the creek lies just ahead, and is reached via a short side trail leading to a small overlook.

Here, the creek slides over bedrock with a small waterfall below.

The main trail continues descending. At the quarter mile, arrive at a side trail leading 200' to a railed viewing area atop the upper falls.

Prominent from this vantage point, to the southwest, is Georgia's Rabun Bald, with the beautiful Blue Valley in the foreground below. This is a great

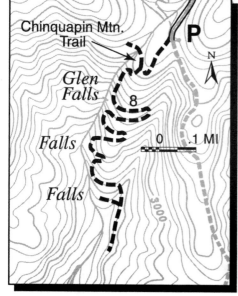

spot for fall foliage shots with the sun high overhead.

From the overlook side trail, the main trail bends left and switchbacks down the mountainside. At .4 of a mile take a 20' side trail to a basal view of the upper falls.

This tier is very beautiful. Especially so in the growing seasons. Swirling veins of quartz stand out against the dark granite. The bedrock is covered in yellow-green lichens.

The main trail turns sharply left here and once again switchbacks into the valley. At .7 of a mile arrive at the base of the middle falls. Hemlock and rhododendron flank its sides.

The main trail continues downstream, level at first, then descending, bending and meandering as it outlines the mountainside. At .85 of a mile arrive at a trail split. A sign at this location points left, towards the Blue Valley, and right, to the Lower Falls. At just over .9 of a mile arrive at the viewing area for the 12' lower falls.

Waterfall on Scaly Mountain

USGS Quadrangle: Scaly Mountain, NC   A "4"
BT, yellow blaze, .3 of a mile, 15 minutes, minor water crossings, moderate-difficult

Note: Best seen after rainfall.

Directions: From the turnoff for Glen Falls, continue on NC 106 for an additional 3.95 miles (5.8 miles total from US 64) to the Osage Mountain Overlook. Park here.

Hike the Bartram Trail north (steps on the north side of NC 106). In 300' cross a small, fern-lined creek. The trail then bends left to climb the hillside. (This mountainside is recovering from a fire. Charred stumps, seen occasion-

ally along the route, attest to this fire. Dense heath has taken over much of the mountainside. The Bartram Trail is narrow through this heath, much like walking between hedgerows. In places, it's hard to see your feet.) With a right bend, round the mountainside, and at just over .2 of a mile cross a small, trickling branch flowing over an outcrop of milky quartz. Slightly over a quarter-mile into the hike, look for a slim, gently-descending path, on the left, leading 100' to a side view of this 15' waterfall. (If you cross a substantial [year-round] creek, you've gone too far and are upstream from the falls).

The fall's rock face has swirling veins of quartz. Aquatic plants decorate the exposure's far side. On the near side, mosses thrive where sheltered from the main flow. The falls are surrounded by dense rhododendron.

Flowers and plants found here, include: foamflower, galax, Mayapple, flame azalea, laurels, sassafras, and small chestnut trees.

Via NC 28 South

Directions: From the intersection of NC 28 South and US 64, in Highlands, drive south on 28 to the following points of interest:

A1. The Lower Satulah Falls Overlook: 3.7 miles.

A2. Blue Valley Road (SR 1618/FS 79) access to Picklesimer Rockhouse Falls: 6.1 miles.

A1. Lower Satulah Falls

USGS Quadrangle: Highlands, NC
Seen from overlook A "3"

This waterfall is seen from an overlook on the west side of NC 28. Look North 70° West and approximately 1500' across the valley for this high and slim beauty. Winter offers the best views and water levels. I stopped here on a summer day and couldn't make them out because of the heavy vegetation and lack of water.

Also visible from the Satulah Overlook is Georgia's Rabun Bald (compass bearing S 70° W) and Satulah Mountain, which is due north. Satulah Mountain has beautiful cliffs and wind-bent trees growing in its fissured, plutonic rock.

A2. Picklesimer Rockhouse Falls

Roads: Graveled   An "8" 35'
USGS Quadrangles: Highlands, Scaly Mtn., NC, in their margins
.6 of a mile, wet spots, no water crossings, moderate

Note: This waterfall is high on the slopes of Little Scaly Mtn. and is therefore best seen after adequate rainfall. I have visited this location several times. My last visit was after a one half to one inch summer rain. High in the drainage and lacking steady rain, there was not much water. My most memorable visit was shortly after rainfall and during a cold spell that made the falls especially beautiful. The cliff was decorated with icicles, some of which were four feet long. Aside from that, the alcove has some of the most ornately grained rock that I've seen. Please wait for adequate rains (winter) to see this waterfall—you'll surely not be disappointed.

Directions: From NC 28, turn right (west) onto SR 1618/FS 79 and drive 4.4 miles to an unmarked Forest Service road on the right. This road is neither numbered on maps, or in the field. Park on the *left* side of FS 79 in the pullout provided, so as to not block the gate.

The fall's path treads the unmarked Forest Service road and in 250' passes a gate. Ascending for just over .15 of a mile, the path then levels. At the

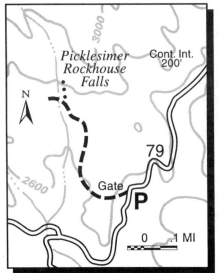

quarter-mile the pathway enters an opening (where there has been recent logging, in the last 5-10 years) and undulates as it descends. After crossing a small, and often dry branch, enter a large wildlife opening (now becoming overgrown). At .45 of a mile exit the opening and reenter the woods. Upon arriving at the fall's branch (the first substantial creek encountered, .5 of a mile into the hike) enter the laurel and hike upstream for 400' to this delicate, veil-like waterfall.

Picklesimer Rockhouse is so named for the shelter its deep overhang provides. Its rock face and overhang have a width of approximately 125'. A monster-sized poplar may stand to its right. Rhododendron flanks its left side and tops the ledge. Mountain magnolia and haircap moss are found here, as well.

Abrams Falls, GSMNP

Cashiers, Sapphire, and Lake Toxaway Areas

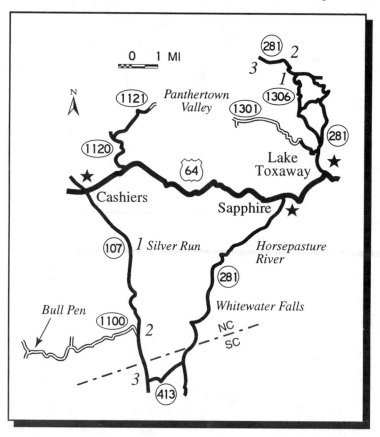

Cashiers Area

Directions: From the intersection of US 64 and NC 107, in Cashiers, drive south on 107 to access the following points of interest:

1. Parking for Silver Run Falls: 4.1 miles.
2. Bull Pen Road (SR 1100), access to the Potholes and Cascades of Bull Pen: 7 miles.
3. Wigington Road (*South Carolina* Hwy. 413, alternate route to Whitewater Falls, see pg. 76): 9.3 miles.

1. Silver Run Falls, Jackson County, NC

Roads: Paved   An "8" 25'
USGS Quadrangle: Cashiers, NC
Trail #435, just over .1 of a mile, 5 minutes, easy, (no hiking map needed)

Note: Bring a hiking stick to help balance yourself on the log serving as the footbridge.

At this location park at the graveled pullout on the left.

The trail enters the woods heading due east from the parking area. Descending initially, in 135' the trail bends right and soon levels in the creek bottom. At 410' cross the creek (a major tributary of the Whitewater River) on a natural footbridge (formed by a dead root or the dead half [trunk] of a still living, double-trunked tree). The trail then turns right and meanders while undulating the remaining 165' to the fall's pool area.

Silver Run photographs best in the diffused light of an overcast day, or in the late afternoon (late spring to early fall) when fully lit by the sun. In winter, with the sun low on the horizon, tall trees on the south side of the plunge pool cast harsh shadows upon the falls.

This is a very beautiful waterfall with a large, blue-green plunge pool.

2. The Potholes and Cascades of Bull Pen

Roads: Graveled   A "10"
Cascades and scenery seen from road or path.

Directions: From NC 107, drive west on Bull Pen Road (passing a potentially confusing SR 1101, on the right at 3.6 miles) for approximately 5.5 miles to the Bull Pen (truss) bridge. Park on the west side of the Chattooga River and walk back to the bridge.

One of the most easily reached points of interest, it is also one of the most scenic. In the distance the Chattooga enters the setting between steep mountainsides, first flowing in peaceful cascades over bedrock and large boulders. As the river nears the bridge, the cascades give way to small falls over ledges and landings with washtub-sized potholes.

3. Wigington Road (SC 413) as above.

Falls of the Panthertown Valley, Jackson County, NC

Roads: Graveled
USGS Quadrangles: Big Ridge, Lake Toxaway, NC
See text for distances, water crossings, moderate-difficult

Dubbed the "Yosemite of the East," this is one of the most beautiful areas that I've encountered. I've spent a great deal of time here, and have only scratched the surface. Fall is my favorite time to visit, provided there has been adequate rainfall to make the waterfalls appealing. This valley is home to some of the finest leaf peeping in the South.

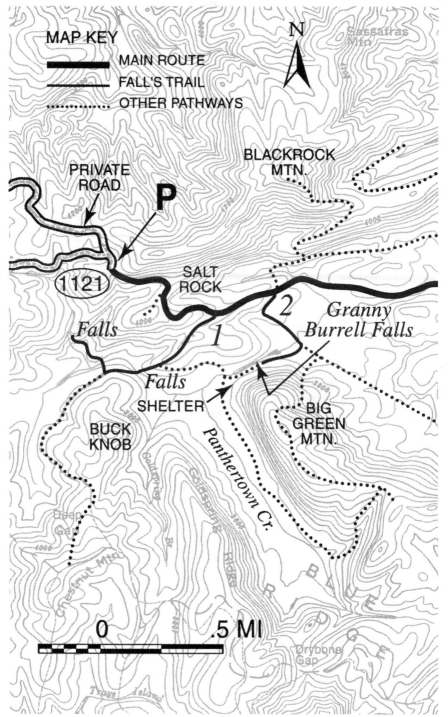

MAP KEY

━━━━━ MAIN ROUTE
───── FALL'S TRAIL
⋯⋯⋯ OTHER PATHWAYS

N

BLACKROCK
MTN.

PRIVATE
ROAD

P

1121

SALT
ROCK

2

*Granny
Burrell Falls*

Falls

1

Falls

SHELTER

BUCK
KNOB

BIG
GREEN
MTN.

Panthertown Cr.

0   .5 MI

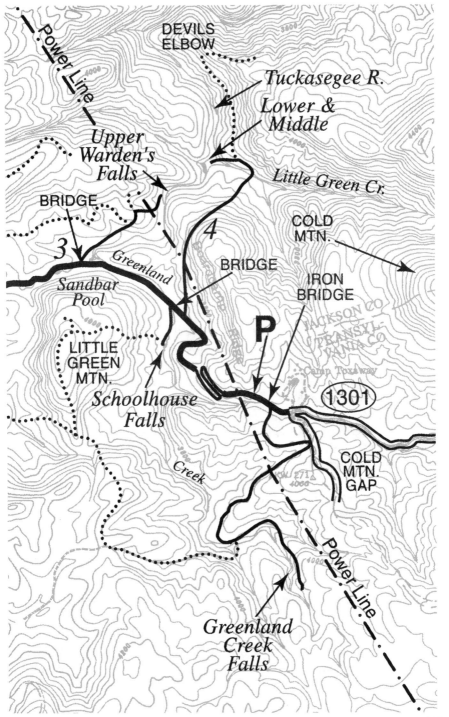

Be prepared for cooler temperatures. Elevations range from 3400', at the Devil's Elbow, to over 4600', atop Cold Mtn. Winters are harsh. Spring arrives late and fall comes at least two weeks early to this upland valley. Foliage peaks by mid-October.

Note: The routes described under this heading are what I feel will become the developed trails of the future. Most of these routes tread old railroad beds or roadbeds. To lessen the impact we have on this beautiful and sensitive area, the shortcuts, manways, and pig trails (too numerous to describe, anyway) have been intentionally left out.

With the hike to Schoolhouse Falls as the baseline, please note the numbered side trails that lead to the valley's other waterfalls. For a back way into the valley, see Greenland Creek Falls and the Cold Mtn. Gap Access at the end of this heading.

Directions: From the intersection of US 64 and NC 107, in Cashiers, drive east on US 64 for 2 miles to Cedar Creek Road (SR 1120). Turn left (north) and drive 2.3 miles to Breedlove Road (SR 1121). Turn right and travel 3.7 miles to the parking area and gate.

Schoolhouse Falls

From the gate, the roadbed leading into Panthertown Valley descends steeply. In approximately 300' sign up at the trail register. The roadbed serving as our trail soon levels then turns uphill while bending right. At .3 of a mile pass through a saddle atop Salt Rock. From an opening, view the beautiful plutonic domes of Big and Little Green mountains, to the east, and Blackrock Mtn. to the northeast. (The plutonic domes of the Panthertown Valley consist of granitoid gneiss.) Schoolhouse Falls lie just beyond Little Green Mtn.

The trail begins to descend once again. Rock exposures and small trees in this area are covered heavily in lichens. At .6 of a mile pass a road leading to the right. (This leads to (**1**) the falls on Frolictown Creek and Double Knob Gap Branch, which will be visited later.) The trail now straightens out and for the moment levels somewhat. At .8 of a mile the road makes a right bend and descends more steeply. At .85 of a mile arrive at a four-way intersection. (The route to the right (**2**) leads to Granny Burrell Falls, which will be visited later, as well.) The route to Schoolhouse Falls continues straight ahead and the roadbed narrows to a wide, single track. At .95 of a mile the treadway levels amongst white pine, hemlock, and rhododendron. A small branch flows alongside the old roadbed here. Now in the valley floor, and undulating, at 1.4 miles the roadbed widens as it joins Panthertown Creek. After crossing a small tributary branch, the next landmark shown on the quadrangle is a large pool (known as Sandbar Pool, 1.7 miles) with a sliding rock on its upper end and a plywood fisherman's cabin on the banks of its lower end. (Look for a piped spring, on the left, just prior to the cabin.) The roadbed makes a left and right jog to circumvent the pool. After being somewhat open, pass under a canopy of white pine. Soon thereafter (1.85 miles), the road forks (see **(3)** Upper Wardens Falls, below). Take the right fork, which immediately crosses Panthertown Creek on an old, wooden auto bridge. (This bridge is in an advanced state of decline, so don't count on it still being intact.) Of special note, in this vicinity, is the occurrence of Fraser fir.

As we enter the drainage of Greenland Creek, the roadbed passes the rhododendron-covered slopes of Little Green Mtn. and through many bogs. At 2.25 miles arrive at a *second* dilapidated auto bridge, this one spanning Greenland Creek (see **(4)** Boardcamp Ridge Access, below). Backtrack 50' and look for a slim path leaving the roadbed and leading upstream. This path meanders for .15 of a mile to Schoolhouse Falls.

A large sandbar precedes the falls. Golf ball to softball-size gneiss gravel is strewn about its sands. The plunge pool is approximately 80' wide and extends 60' out from the falls. Full of rock and clear, the pool shimmers a sunlit golden green. Alder, birch, and hemlock reside on its sandbars. The falls are 15' high, total, consisting of a 10' drop preceded by a 5' cascade. As well, they are approximately 15' wide during average flow.

They are best photographed on an overcast day, in the growing season. Early morning or late afternoon, when the sun is low, also works well. In winter, lens flare is a problem here, as the sun sweeps low across the sky directly behind the falls.

1. Falls on Frolictown Creek and Double Knob Gap Branch

From the main trail, the side trail (an old roadbed) leads level then slightly uphill and in 600' passes the site of an old homestead. Topping out and leveling, the trail soon descends at a moderate rate and passes an old road that intersects from the left. At .45 of a mile arrive at a ford of Frolictown Creek. Backtrack 70' and descend the steep slope to access the base of the falls.

To reach the falls of Double Knob Gap Branch, return to the main trail and cross Frolictown Creek. The trail ascends and soon levels. After a slight descent, at .15 of a mile (from Frolictown Creek), cross a small, wet-weather branch. In 50' look *for* and *take* a barely-discernible path leading north northwest into the doghobble and woods. (The route may be flagged.) In 170', in a single bound, hop Frolictown Creek. Ascend the creek's steep channel and north bank. (There may be a rope to assist in pulling one's self up the slope.) Forty feet from the crossing the faint path splits both left and right. Take the path on the left (initially leading west). The path soon resumes its north northwesterly trend. Two hundred thirty feet from the creek crossing arrive beside the falls branch (which is on the left). The path now turns slightly uphill to follow the creek upstream. Meandering through the rhododendron, often out of sight of the creek, at 765' arrive at a point of land where the path splits once again. Take the descending path, on the left, for 45' to the bedrock viewing area of this 60'-high waterfall.

The 80'-wide edifice has water occupying 25' of its width. Most of its waters flow to the extreme right side, in a narrow, ribbonlike flow. Waters to the immediate left flow wide and thin, and as clear as glass. After this initial fall, the creek's waters gather into a single flow and slide right to left in an uneven cascade of 20′ (in height) then are directed straight towards the viewer. There are beautiful maples to its left and hemlocks to its right. White pine and a double-trunked hemlock top it off. Despite its lack of water, the setting is very beautiful and made more so by fall's colors.

2. Granny Burrell Falls

Leaving the main trail with a compass bearing of S 20° W, the road to Granny Burrell Falls makes a bend right, traveling level for approximately 125′. With a slight descent, the roadbed straightens and at 350′ bends left. At .1 of a mile look for a brick barbecue and fire ring approximately 75′ to the trail's left. The route now meanders through a level area, then at .15 of a mile enters an opening with Big Green Mtn. looming to the south. At the quarter-mile arrive alongside Panthertown Creek. The creek flows straight towards the viewer then makes a sharp bend east (a very scenic setting). In 150′ cross an old, wooden auto bridge over Panthertown Creek. The fall's rushing waters can be heard upstream, in this vicinity, when the leaves are off. At .3 of a mile, tread a sandy stretch and with two water-filled depressions straight ahead, look for a slim path leading right. Take this side path and soon tread an old roadbed leading alongside Panthertown Creek. The path soon narrows into a well-defined, single-lane treadway. At .4 of a mile the path is forced onto the creek's bedrock. The falls lie 100′ upstream. (This is a hazardous area in the wintertime, because of ground water seeping, then freezing on the bedrock.)

The fall's rock face is approximately 40′ wide. Panthertown Creek enters the scene through a shallow, U-shaped, bedrock channel, then flows over rounded bedrock, shoaling as a 15′-high fall. A small, shallow pool lies at its base. Laurel and rhododendron grow on its flanks. Small white pines form the backdrop. Look for a drill bit atop the falls, on the right.

The creek exits the pool and shoals over banded gneiss for approximately 100′, then slips into a much larger pool. A hardwood-covered sandbar contains its waters and makes for one of the valley's most colorful fall sights.

3. Upper Warden's Falls

From the fork, the roadbed heads northeasterly, ascending while entering the Tuckasegee River drainage. In .3 of a mile cross a small creek flowing through a rock buildup. At .4 of a mile the roadbed is intersected from the left by a woodland road similar to the one we tread. One hundred twenty-five feet from this intersection, while in a left bend, look *for* and *take* a slim path on the right (compass bearing, N 80° E) that leaves the roadbed. In 30′ the path forks. Take the left (north) fork for an additional .15 of a mile to the bedrock viewing area at the base of the falls. (Use caution atop the potentially slick bedrock.)

The falls are 30′ wide at the top and fan out to a width of 45′. The left side slides and sends a small roostertail into the air, while the right side slides 20′ then makes an 8′ drop into a small pool. The bedrock sports minor potholes.

4. Boardcamp Ridge Access (Lower and Middle Warden's Falls)

Cross Greenland Creek via the second bridge and hike southeasterly for 245' to a point where an old road intersects from the left (north). Starting our distances anew, take this route, which ascends Boardcamp Ridge, and in .35 of a mile pass under the power line. At .45 of a mile top the ridge line and descend into the drainage of Little Green Creek. Upon crossing Little Green (.85 of a mile), the trail generally parallels its unseen north side while heading northwest (downstream). Just shy of a mile, look for a side path which forks left (N 70° W) to tread an old roadbed. Take this descending pathway for 540' to the top of the sliding, Lower Warden's Falls. (Like Granny Burrell Falls, this is a hazardous area in the wintertime, because of ground water seeping, then freezing on the bedrock.)

The Tuckasegee makes a 90° left turn here then shoals for 100' over shallow bedrock that is covered in bright green algaes (in springtime). At their base, the river bends left flowing towards the Devil's Elbow. Fir, weirdly-shaped pines, and lots of large boulders lend to this beautiful setting.

The route to Middle Falls leaves the Lower Fall's bedrock viewing area, at the top of Lower Falls, and enters the woods via a tunnellike opening (while heading south). In 110' arrive in the vicinity of a fire ring, which is on the left. The route now turns right (westerly) and winds for 200' through the rhododendron towards the Tuckasegee and the Middle Fall's viewing area.

Middle Falls is approximately 20' high (shoaling 30' at a 45° angle). After moderate rainfall, water occupies the left half of its 30 to 50'-wide bedrock exposure. In winter, a sheet of ice covers the otherwise barren bedrock to their right. The falls slip quietly into a large, placid pool, bounded by a sandy beach. Beautiful, moss-draped trees overhang the pool's tannin-stained waters. Look for evidence of beaver activity. The falls are best photographed on an overcast day.

Greenland Creek Falls (Holly Falls)

Cold Mtn. Road (SR 1301) is the east access, or what I consider the back way into the Panthertown Valley. It also provide~ ~e easiest access to Greenland Creek Falls. Apply the followi~ closed ~ to the Lake Toxaway portion of the area map.

Directions: From the inte~ ~ 281 *North,* just east of the Lake Toxaway Dam, dri~ ~or .85 of a mile. Turn left onto Cold Mtn. Road (SR 1301) and ~ .1 miles to the parking area at Cold Mtn. Gap. (The maintained graveled road ends at 5.9 miles and gives way to a single-lane dirt road.)

From the parking area, retrace the inbound road for 340', to the east side of the iron bridge (crossed enroute to the parking area). From this point, hike Cold Mtn. Road *east* for 30' and look for a slim path entering the woods on the right (south) side of the road. Bending in reverse "S" fashion, the path ascends while heading south. At 740' a slim path splits right and leads towards the power line. At 885' pass a survey marker while entering the National Forest. In 40' the path turns left to tread a Duke Power access road. With a graveled road dead ahead (.35 of a mile) arrive at a gate. To the immediate right, or south side of the gate, enter the woods on a slim path. This woodland path meanders *alongside*, and soon treads *upon* an old roadbed, in a southwesterly direction. At the half mile, pass under the power line. At .9 of a mile a side path intersects from the west. Now on lower ground, Greenland Creek is heard but for the moment remains unseen. Enter and pass through an opening (1.05 miles). On its far side, look *for* and *take* a path on the *left* (N 80° E), that reenters the woods. (As information, there are two old roadbeds that cross Greenland Creek at this opening. The first is on the right, as the opening is entered, the second is across the opening and to the right of the correct pathway.)

White pines soon give way to tunnels of rhododendron and laurel. After crossing several small creeks, while meandering through the doghobble, galax, and rhododendron hell, rejoin Greenland Creek (1.35 miles) and hike up its rocky overflow area. Soon thereafter, arrive at the boulder-strewn viewing area for Greenland Creek Falls.

The falls are 35' high, total, consisting of a 25' upper tier and an 8' lower tier. The upper tier slides then falls over the left side of the 25'-wide bedrock exposure, landing unseen on a bedrock ledge. The creek resumes its run, descending towards the viewer, then makes a shoaling, 8' slide to the right side of the *now* 60'-wide exposure. Boulders litter and fill the tannin-stained pool at their base. Fir and pine top them, while rhododendron and laurel flank its sides.

Cold Mtn. Gap Access

If entering the valley from Cold Mtn. Gap, here are the highlights encountered enroute to the tie-in, with the above-mentioned Boardcamp Ridge Access and the second bridge (near Schoolhouse Falls):

- 0.0: Iron gate.
- 100': Road to right leads up Cold Mtn. (stay left).
- .1 of a mile: Old gate.
- .2 of a mile: Weather station.
- .2 to .55 of a mile: Switchbacks descending into valley.
- .8 of a mile: Trail split, route to right (4) Boardcamp Ridge Access to Lower and Middle Warden's Falls (see above).
- .85 of a mile: Tie-in with bridge over Greenland Creek, near Schoolhouse Falls.

For more detailed information on the geology, and other trails in this area, purchase a copy of *A Guide's Guide to Panthertown Valley, by Burt Kornegay*. This map/guide may be purchased from Slickrock Expeditions, P.O. Box 1214, Cullowhee, NC, 28723.

Sapphire Area

Falls on the Horsepasture River, Transylvania County, NC

Roads: Paved   Allow at least one-half day for visit.
USGS Quadrangle: Reid, NC
1.85 miles to Stairway Falls, water crossings, moderate to difficult

Directions: From the intersection of US 64 and NC 281 South, in the community of Sapphire, drive south on 281 for .9 of a mile to a pullout on the left.

The first portion of this popular hike has been rerouted to avoid the dangers present at Drift Falls. Drift Falls (a.k.a. "Bust Your Butt Falls") had become a safety concern because of its use as a water slide. It became a party place with

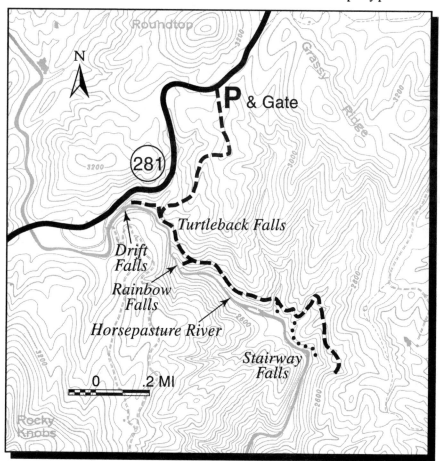

revelers littering its banks, destroying the vegetation, and blocking traffic on NC 281. For those familiar with the territory, the new route bisects the old trail between Drift and Turtleback Falls.

From the gate, hike an old logging road that heads generally south. In .2 of a mile pass to the left of a small knoll. At the quarter mile, after rounding the knoll, the trail starts descending. At .3 of a mile arrive at a confusing split. Take the right fork. At the half mile, pass the Forest Service gate and sign stating, "Road Closed." The river is soon heard resonating through the woods. Descending more steeply, pass a primitive campsite situated on a level spot to the left (.7 of a mile). Three fourths of a mile into the hike, intersect the old trail at river level.

The route to the right leads upstream to Drift Falls. This will be visited later (see below*).

Hike downstream. In just over 200′ the river churns white as you near the top of Turtleback Falls. Visible downstream, from alongside Turtleback, where the river disappears, is the top of Rainbow Falls, approximately .1 of a mile away. Pass a boulder outcrop to the left of Turtleback and cross a small footbridge over a tributary branch. The trail now bends sharply right to continue following the river downstream. At just over .85 of a mile arrive at a frontal view of Turtleback Falls.

Turtleback is approximately 15′ high—if you count the cascades above it. This whitewater slide shoots over a broken and undercut bedrock shelf and spills into a deep plunge pool. Making a 90° right bend, and heading for Rainbow Falls, the river churns white as its exit is constricted by boulders and bedrock.

Continuing downstream, at .9 of a mile, look for a side path leading 100′ to the top area of Rainbow Falls. (Extreme caution is advised at the fall's unprotected exposures. In winter, the bedrock may be ice covered and treacherous.) This is a churning, violent waterfall. The river foams and leaps bright white, filling the air with mist, as it makes a 150′ plunge. In winter, drifting clouds of mist coat the nearby trees in a crystal glaze. The railed walkway, on the left side, and the base access trail, both seen far below, may be drenching wet and ice covered.

The main trail now descends steeply alongside Rainbow Falls. As the trail exits the woods and levels, a frontal view of the falls is presented. In this vicinity, the base access trail leaves the main trail, and switchbacks while leading 400′ to the lower viewing area. Rainbow Falls best shows its power when fully sunlit, from around 9 to 11 a.m. And yes, a rainbow does hang in the mist, under the right conditions. (See the introduction for those conditions.)

Return to the main trail and pass the railed, frontal view of the falls. The ground is soggy from perpetual mist.

The trail continues downstream, reentering the woods and descending steeply from this point. At 1.15 miles the route becomes a more gently descending, meandering, and undulating one, that soon makes a close pass to the river. At 1.2 miles look for a side path descending to a beautiful, riverside view.

The river enters the scene in 5 to 6' cascades, over and through large boulders. Downstream, the river's course is filled with boulders. Its sunlit waters reflect silver and bright white, in a dramatic mountain setting. Alder trees are present on its banks and galax grows heavily on its inland slopes.

From this point, the river and trail run more closely. Often under a canopy of rhododendron, the trail soon passes a small, primitive campsite and shortly thereafter, a prominent bedrock outcrop jutting towards the river. In passing, the trail descends steeply once again. At 1.45 miles, as you enter a woodland clearing, the trail levels. A primitive campsite and fire ring lie just over 200' ahead. A large (10-15' wide), unnamed creek flows to the campsite's far side. The trail makes a right and left jog and crosses this creek on steppingstones. (In the rainy months you may get your feet wet here.)

The main trail now turns immediately uphill and in 50' is intersected by a path that veers 45° to the right. (This leads 200' to a riverside camping area.) Stay left, and at just over 1.55 miles the trail turns sharply left to outline a dry hollow. In .1 of a mile, after having ascended steeply out of that hollow, the trail bends sharply left to enter a much deeper hollow. In this bend look for a side path on the right (720' from the last creek crossing) that bisects the main trail at a 90° angle. This leads to Stairway Falls. Blink your eyes and you might miss this side path.

Descending a point of land (the lower crest of a ridge), the side path steepens as it nears a riverside campsite (1.7 miles). At the campsite, look for a slim path running 30 to 40' inland and leading down river. This path immediately enters the rhododendron thicket and at 1.75 miles crosses a small creek. The path then winds through the thicket and arrives beside the audible but unseen upper reaches of Stairway Falls. Continuing downstream, the pathway steepens considerably as you near the base of the falls. At 1.85 miles arrive at the rocky, sandy, and driftwood-littered viewing area just downstream from the base.

Broadening as it descends, the falls run approximately 200', dropping a total of 60' in 6 major steps. A large, blue-green pool eddies at its base. The river bends 90° right to flow almost due south as it exits the pool.

*Hike upstream for 800' to the Drift Falls viewing area.

The falls are approximately 30' high and slide, foaming white, for 40 to 50' over bedrock. Twenty-five feet wide at the top, the waterfall fans out to a width of 60' at the base.

Whitewater Falls Scenic Area - Falls on Corbin Creek, Transylvania County, NC

Roads: Paved   Whitewater A "10+" easy to first viewpoint
Corbin Creek A "6" 70', water crossings, difficult
USGS Quadrangle: Cashiers, NC
US Fee Area, Daily fee good for date of purchase at other FS sites.
Day use only, picnic tables, restrooms

Note: The best and safest views are from the overlooks at the end of the paved trail. Behind Whitewater's beautiful facade lurks great danger. Fifteen people who couldn't resist that closer look, have lost their lives here. I do not advise any visitation to the top area. There are no developed trails to the top. The Foothills Trail does make a close pass enroute to the Whitewater River above the falls. Those directions are contained in the text below. Whitewater Falls cannot be seen or approached from the Foothills Trail (the trail leading down to the river from the overlooks).

Directions: See the directions to the falls on the Horsepasture River, and continue south on NC 281 for an additional 7.7 miles. The Whitewater Fall's parking area is on the left.

Alternate directions: From the intersection of US 64 and NC 107, in Cashiers, drive south on 107 for 9.3 miles to Wigington Road (*South Carolina* Hwy. 413, sign: "Whitewater Falls"). Turn left and drive 2.2 miles to NC 281 (stop sign). Turn left and continue 1.15 miles to a right turn which leads to the parking area .2 of a mile away.

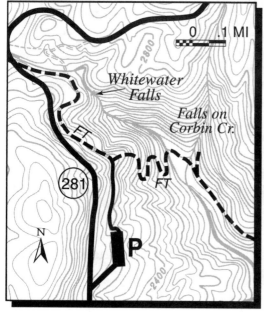

At 411', Whitewater Falls is thought to be the highest waterfall in the eastern US. Located in a most rustic gorge, the falls look as if plucked from a western setting. Beautiful any time of the year, and heavily visited because of its easy access, the falls and gorge are exceptional in autumn— provided there has been adequate rainfall. I was fortunate enough to visit when the leaves were at their peak and while water levels were moderate (just right). I've never seen them more beautiful.

This powerful waterfall is best seen and photographed during midday when the sun is high enough to brightly light *it*, and the gorge.

From the parking area, the paved trail leads at an easy to moderate rate for .2 of a mile to the main overlook. The white-blazed Foothills Trail is encountered here. This leads both left, towards the Whitewater River above the falls, and right, descending very steeply, to another (better) overlook, then onward to the Falls on Corbin Creek.

Whitewater River above the falls

From the overlook, the Foothills Trail leads uphill at a moderate rate for .15 of a mile where it then tops out and descends. In places, this stretch of trail is badly rutted, rocky, and has exposed culverts. At just over .3 of a mile pass by the top area. The trail descends from this point, at an easy to moderate rate, for approximately .1 of a mile to the Whitewater River, upstream from the falls.

Lower Overlook and Falls on Corbin Creek

From the main overlook, the Foothills Trail descends steeply via steps and landings for 250' to the lower overlook area. A slim path leads atop boulders to a grand view of the falls and gorge.

From the lower overlook area, the Foothills Trail descends steeply over rubble and hundreds of uneven steps as it switchbacks to the Whitewater River. At .3 of a mile look for a trickling branch in a steep and deep hollow. Solomon's seal, jack-in-the-pulpit, foamflower, and ferns reside under the canopy of this predominantly hardwood forest. The trail crosses and recrosses the just-mentioned branch enroute to river level. Upon arriving at the Whitewater River (.7 of a mile), the trail turns downstream for approximately 50 to 60', passing over rubble and through a crevice, which is formed by a large boulder, on the left, and lesser ones, on the right. The route then turns left and crosses the river on an iron footbridge (helicoptered into place in 1995). (A massive log, with a handrail, served as the footbridge here, until washed away. Given the history of prior structures, this new bridge may be missing, as well, as flash floods take most everything in their path. If the bridge is missing, no attempt should be made to wade the swift river.) Upon crossing, the trail then turns left, atop a boulder supporting the span, descends, then turns immediately right and enters the woods through a narrow opening in the treeline. In less than .1 of a mile arrive at Corbin Creek. Upstream, just out of view, is a beautiful waterfall on Corbin Creek. Hike upstream for approximately 50' and find a shallow crossing. (The rocks are too slick for rock hopping. A log footbridge once spanned the creek here. Hopefully, you'll find it replaced.) After crossing, hike upstream through the rhododendron and hemlocks for approximately 200' to the base area.

Lake Toxaway Area

Directions: From the intersection of US 64 and NC 281 *North,* just east of the Lake Toxaway Dam, drive north on 281 for 1.45 miles to Slick Fisher Road (SR 1306). Turn left and drive 4.55 miles and reintersect NC 281 near the now vacant and unmarked Big Pisgah Church. As you turn left (north) onto NC 281 (now a graveled road) zero your odometer and travel the following distances to:

1. The parking area for Dismal Falls[1]: .35 of a mile.
2. FS 5070, access to Mill Branch[1]: 1.1 miles.
3. Owens Gap: 2.3 miles.

[1] These waterfalls are located in the Pisgah N. F. They are listed here because of their close proximity to points of interest in the Nantahala N. F.

1. Unnamed Waterfall, Lower and Upper Dismal Falls, Transylvania County, NC

Roads: Graveled   A "3" 35', & A Pair of "10's" 35 and 60' respectively
USGS Quadrangle: Lake Toxaway, NC   Allow at least one-half day.
No official trail, 1.7 miles to Upper Dismal, water crossings, moderate to difficult

Note: Upper Dismal Falls may be seen, in winter, from a point on NC 281, .05 of a mile from Owens Gap. At that point, with a compass bearing of S 15° W, look for them approximately 1/3 of the way down the valley that separates Shelton Pisgah and Big Pisgah mtns.

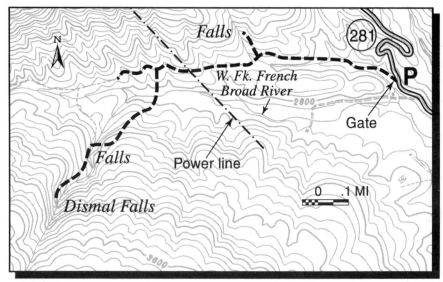

THE RAMSAY CASCADES,
GREAT SMOKY MTNS. NP

MAMIYA 645 SUPER, 45 MM LENS @ f/22
FUJI VELVIA EXPOSED FOR 1 SECOND

FALL COLOR AT GRANNY BURRELL FALLS,
PANTHERTOWN VALLEY, NC

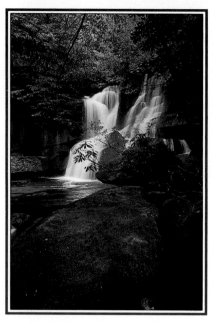

CEDAR ROCK FALLS, NC

MIDDLE FALLS,
SNOWBIRD CREEK, NC

LONG CREEK FALLS,
CHATTOOGA RIVER CORRIDOR, SC

WILDCAT FALLS,
SLICKROCK CREEK,
NC, TN

WHITEWATER FALLS, NC

C

MOUSE CREEK FALLS,
GSMNP

CASCADE FALLS,
GSMNP

CASCADES OF BULL PEN,
CHATTOOGA RIVER

UPPER DISMAL FALLS, NC

D

LINVILLE FALLS,
BLUE RIDGE PARKWAY, NC

MAMIYA 645 SUPER, 55 MM LENS @ f/22
FUJI VELVIA EXPOSED FOR 1/60TH SEC.

E

CHAUGA RIVER,
CHAU RAM PARK, SC

SPOONAUGER FALLS,
CHATTOOGA RIVER, SC

CATHEY'S CREEK, NC

YELLOW BRANCH, SC

F

RAVEN CLIFF FALLS, SC

GREENLAND CREEK FALLS, NC

G

SPRUCE FLATS FALLS, GSMNP

MAMIYA 645 SUPER, 45 MM LENS @ f/16
KODAK 100SW EXPOSED FOR 1 SECOND

H

Park on the east shoulder of the road, in the space provided. Directly across the road (west) is a gated logging road that serves as the trail.

Initially, the route is rutted and somewhat rugged. As well, it crosses a half dozen creeks and passes through several wildlife openings. At .5 of a mile look for a side path to the right. This leads 450' to the base of the unnamed falls.

Even though there is not alot of water here, this is a beautiful waterfall that falls from a bold, 60'-wide rock edifice. At the time of my last visit, there was a hemlock atop the lower tier that hung precariously over the creek, before shooting straight up. Return to the main trail and continue westerly.

Just shy of a mile, pass under a small power line. Two-tenths of a mile from this landmark, the old roadbed peters out amongst a stand of white pines. At this location look *for* and *take* a faint path that leaves the roadbed at a 90° angle (south) heading towards the West Fork of the French Broad River. In 180' cross the river (more like a creek than river). Seventy-five feet from this crossing, the route turns southwesterly and ascends into the cove of Dismal Creek. In just over .1 of a mile arrive at the base of Lower Dismal Falls.

The lower falls are a beauty, spilling from ledge to ledge in a three-tier dance down the bedrock. Its sounds are soothingly hypnotic and would make the perfect white noise CD. Its waters collect briefly at the base then are channeled to the right into a narrow chute and spill downstream. With the easy part behind us, when you're rested we'll carry on.

To reach Upper Dismal Falls, cross the creek (below the lower falls) at its narrowest point, and ascend the steep bank on its west side. About 100' away intersect an overgrown firebreak or logging road. (All that remains of this cut in the earth is a swale and gully.) Hike this steep cut upstream for .3 of a mile. Look to the left for a glimpse of the falls or the rock alcove that houses them. Wade through the rhododendron thicket down to creek level. Hike the creek upstream to the base area of this pristine jewel of nature.

Dismal Falls consists of a sheer, delicate drop of 60' from a massive rock ledge. The shallow pool at its base is flanked by large hardwoods as well as hemlock.

There is nothing dismal about it. Even the somewhat arduous hike is a pleasant adventure.

2. Unnamed Branch, Mill Branch Drainage, Transylvania County, NC

Roads: Graveled   A "3"
USGS Quadrangle: Lake Toxaway, NC
.2 of a mile, easy

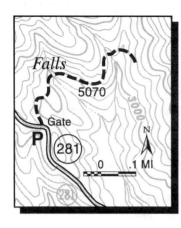

Park in the pullout located here. The hike begins at the gate.

Hike FS 5070 for .2 of a mile. This small but very pretty, wet-weather waterfall lies to the left. During the growing season it is obscured from view. The left side of the creek offers the best access. A careful wade through the briars and other waist-high growth is necessary to see them close-up.

3. Owens Gap (as above).

Looking Glass Falls

Pisgah National Forest

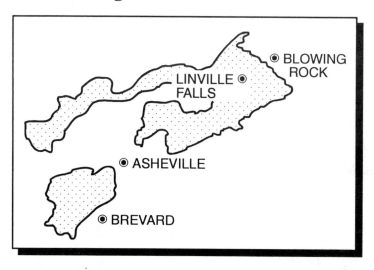

The Pisgah National Forest is comprised of 495,000 acres in western North Carolina. The name "Pisgah" was taken from the Biblical mountain from which Moses saw the promised land. Legend has it, that in 1776, Rev. James Hall, a Presbyterian minister, named the mountain while in the region fighting the Cherokee. Upon viewing the French Broad River valley, from atop what is now known as Mount Pisgah, he was reminded of the promised land that Moses had described from the mountain bearing the same name.

The Pisgah National Forest is where scientific forestry was first practiced in America. In 1889, George W. Vanderbilt began purchasing land for his country estate, "Biltmore House." Mr. Vanderbilt expanded his holdings to include Mount Pisgah. He envisioned an estate that perpetuated itself from the sale of forest products raised in "Pisgah Forest." Mr. Vanderbilt chose forestry expert, Gifford Pinchot, to manage this endeavor. In 1895, Dr. Carl Schenck, replaced Mr. Pinchot who had gone on to be the first head of the US Forest Service. Dr. Schenck started the Biltmore Forest School, in 1898, to teach modern forestry techniques. The school graduated some 367 students before ceasing operations in 1914.

In 1968, Congress passed the "Cradle of Forestry in America Act" which set aside 6400 acres to commemorate forest conservation in America. A visitor center is located north of Sliding Rock on US 276 (see pages 89 and 96). Here also, you'll find the restored schoolhouse and living quarters of the Biltmore Forest School, as well as an old sawmill and a narrow-gauge locomotive, which was used to haul logs out of the mountain's hollows.

The Land of Waterfalls
Transylvania County, N. Carolina

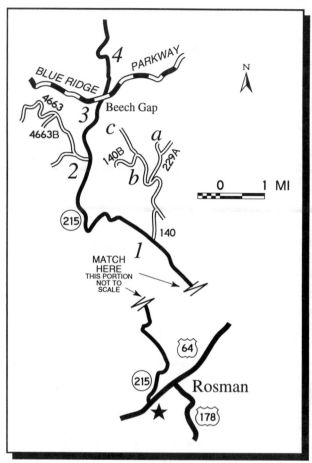

Seventy inches of annual rainfall, and some pretty hefty mountainsides, make this area a "Waterfall Walkers Paradise." With over 200 waterfalls (many on private property), Transylvania County touts itself as, "The Land of Waterfalls." Looking Glass and Whitewater Falls are the centerpieces. With their great beauty and easy accessibility, both are heavily visited.

For those who are willing to travel graveled or dirt roads, and endure hikes of varying difficulty, there are ample rewards in the area, too. Courthouse and Dismal Falls, both knockouts, require hikes at the ability extremes (the former—easy, the latter—somewhat arduous). In most cases, when there are crowds at the "popular spots" you can visit the "lesser knowns" in peace and relative solitude.

The waterfalls in the text of pages 83 through 96, unless otherwise noted, are located in Transylvania County.

Rosman - Beech Gap Area

Directions: From the intersection of US 64 and NC 215, near Rosman, drive north on 215 to the following points of interest:

1. FS 140, access to the falls on the N. Fork of the French Broad River: (a) the Falls on Chestnut Creek; (b) Courthouse Falls; and (c) the Upper Falls on Courthouse Creek: 10.55 miles.
2. FS 4663, access to Dill Falls[2]: 14.55 miles.
3. The Blue Ridge Parkway at Beech Gap: 17.15 miles.
4. The parking area for Wildcat Falls: 17.95 miles.

[2] Dill Falls is located in the Nantahala N. F. Because of its close proximity to the Pisgah N. F., it is listed here.

1a. Falls on Chestnut Creek

Roads: Graveled/High Clearance   A "4" 20'
USGS Quadrangle: Sam Knob, NC
.9 of a mile, moderate

Directions: Turn right (north) onto FS 140 and drive 2.7 miles to FS 229A (Kiesee Creek Road) which is on the right. Park here.

From the gate, hike Kiesee Creek Road which ascends while making a long

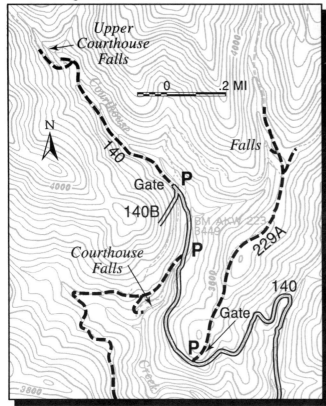

right bend. At 425' the roadbed levels and beautiful mountains become visible to the east. Treading the crest of Chestnut Ridge, at .2 of a mile, the balsam dotted mountaintops of Pisgah Ridge become visible to the north. An easy landmark to pick out, is the dark, craggy rock of the Devil's Courthouse, on the Blue Ridge Parkway. At just over a half mile, the roadbed tops out, descends, then soon thereafter levels. At .8 of a mile the road forks. Take the left fork. Chestnut Creek can be heard, to the left, in this vicinity. Heading due north, in just under 200' encounter a couple of jeep-blocking mounds. At .9 of a mile look for a slim path washed into the shoulder of the road, leading down towards the creek. Descend this path, and in approximately 150' arrive at the viewing area.

The falls are viewed from a point approximately 70' downstream from the base. The cove is hardwood filled, dominated by poplar. Laurel, rhododendron, and hemlock form the creekside understory, with thick doghobble present on the forest floor.

This untouched waterfall should be especially beautiful when the rhododendron is in bloom.

1b. Courthouse Falls

Roads: Graveled   A "10+"
USGS Quadrangle: Sam Knob, NC
Trail #'s 129/130, .3 of a mile, easy-moderate

Note: This trail has wet spots even in the dry season.

This beautiful waterfall resides in a dreamlike setting and is one that I keep coming back to, time after time. There is so much beauty here that it escapes being captured on a single frame of film, or being fully appreciated in a single visit. Place this waterfall high on your list of priorities.

Directions: See the directions to the Falls on Chestnut Creek and continue north on FS 140 for .4 of a mile to the pullouts (trail parking) on the north side of the bridge that crosses Courthouse Creek. The Summey Cove Trail (which leads to the falls) begins 25' north of the downstream side of the bridge. There may be a carsonite stake stating, "to Courthouse Falls."

The trail enters the woods and immediately passes jeep-blocking boulders. Routed atop an old roadbed, the trail treads alongside Courthouse Creek. At 400', in a rocky wash, tread a boardwalk. At .2 of a mile, the sound of rushing water indicates that the gorge suddenly deepens. The falls may be seen from the trail in this vicinity, through winter's open woods. Giving the steep-sided gorge a wide berth, the trail makes a right bend. At just under .3 of a mile, with a sharp left, the orange-blazed fall's trail leaves the Summey Cove Trail to descend into the gorge. At .35 of a mile arrive at the base of the falls. As you approach, you'll understand why I so often visit this area.

Courthouse Creek flows through a "V" in the rock face, slides down a chute, then slips into a very deep pool. Large hardwoods create a canopy that deeply shades the alcove, giving the crystal-clear plunge pool a deep, blue-green tint. The rounded rock wall, on the left, weeps nutrients to dozens of aquatic plants. Beautiful mosses and lichens adorn the wall on the right.

1c. Upper Falls on Courthouse Creek

Roads: Graveled   A "2" 15' & 6' respectively
USGS Quadrangle: Sam Knob, NC
Courthouse Trail #128, .7 of a mile, easy-moderate

Directions: See the directions to Courthouse Falls and continue north on FS 140 for .2 of a mile and arrive at a point where FS 140B, on the left, and FS 140, which continues on the right, are gated. Park here.

From the gate, the roadbed ascends at an easy to moderate rate. Initially paralleling rhododendron-lined Courthouse Creek at a distance of approximately 30', at just under .2 of a mile the roadbed veers away from the creek. At just over .3 of a mile the creek once again comes in sight and the route soon passes a moss-covered, boulder outcrop on the left. At .6 of a mile the cove's hardwood-covered slopes narrow significantly and the roadbed and beautiful, tumbling creek are forced close together. Seven tenths of a mile into the hike arrive at the road's end. The creek forks here, as well. The sliding, 15' lower falls are seen straight up the creek's left fork, approximately 100' from this point.

Look for the Courthouse Trail, on the left, leading steeply up the hillside. (If the trail's carsonite stake is missing—while standing at the fire ring, at the road's end, the proper route is found with a compass bearing of N 80° W.)

Hike this trail and in 85' (from the end of the road) take a doghobble-lined *path* leading right. One-hundred ten feet from this point, arrive at the top of the lower falls.

This waterfall has a run of 35', and a small pool above it. The bedrock is very smooth here. Water sculpted, it shows attractive quartz veins.

Approximately 50' upstream is a very beautiful, 6' waterfall that spills into a small pool. This pool extends 25' towards the viewer. Out of this pool the creek splits. Flowing around a high spot in the bedrock the waters rejoin in a slide to the lower falls.

2. Dill Falls, Jackson County, NC

Roads: High Clearance   A "4"*
USGS Quadrangle: Sam Knob, NC
.2 of a mile, 10 minutes, moderate

Directions: From the intersection of NC 215 and FS 4663, near Cold Spring Gap, take 4663 leading west. Initially passing through private land, at .55 of a mile the road forks. Veer right and continue for a total of 1.9 miles, to a point where 4663 starts steeply up the mountainside. At this location look for the unimproved FS 4663B, on the left. Drive this road for .6 of a mile. (*This road may have deep mudholes near its end, but is generally in good condition.

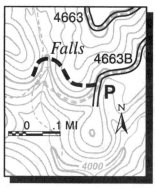

If carefully driven, most high-clearance vehicles can negotiate this road.) As you enter a clearing and turnaround (the site of recent logging activity), look to the right (WNW) for a road that crosses several jeep-blocking mounds while leading uphill. (This road serves as the pathway to the falls.) Park here.

Initially encountering the rolling jeep mounds, the roadbed climbs steeply. At 600' the route tops out, levels, and soon descends into the cove housing the falls. At 860' arrive at the top area. Look for a steep side path, leading downhill, through the waist-deep underbrush. Take this path for approximately 80' to the fall's viewing area.

Dill Falls is of the sliding variety, over exposed bedrock. This exposure is approximately 25' wide. The falls are 20 to 25' high, the last 5' of which free-falls, splashing onto ornately grained bedrock. Most of its flow is to the exposure's right side. During normal flow, the creek occupies 5 to 8' of the width of the rock face.

3. The Blue Ridge Parkway (as above).

4. Wildcat Falls, Haywood County, NC

Roads: Paved   A "3" 60'
USGS Quadrangle: Sam Knob, NC
Trail #350, .65 of a mile, 20 minutes, easy-moderate

Note: Best seen after rainfall or when iced over in winter.

Directions: From the intersection of NC 215 and the Blue Ridge Parkway, drive north on 215 for .8 of a mile to a small parking area, on the right. (This parking area is somewhat obscured, as it is below road level.) Park here.

Because there is no trail marker at the parking area, I have chosen the crossing of Bubbling Spring Branch as the hike's fixed beginning point. To reach this point, hike the descending access road for just over 250' to the creek crossing.

The Flat Laurel Creek Trail crosses Bubbling Spring Branch and turns left, treading an old logging railroad bed. At 625' cross the rocky overflow of a small, unnamed tributary. Upstream, approximately 40' away, are two small, wet-weather waterfalls. (This creek flows through a culvert, but in overflowing has washed the roadbed exposing alot of rock.) The trail now begins ascending and at 800' narrows. Leveling, at .2 of a mile, the trail becomes less rocky while passing through laurel and rhododendron. Just ahead, to the trail's left, are stately Fraser firs with over-the-top views of the beautiful, heath-

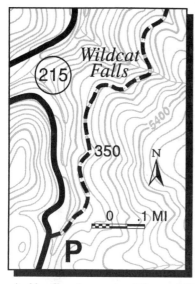

surrounded bedrock of Fork Ridge. Three-tenths of a mile into the hike, the trail plies the depths of a small cove. In a deep cut, at the half-mile point, round a right bend whose slopes support a heavy growth of laurel. In a shallow cove, at just under .6 of a mile, look for a beautiful, moss-covered rock slide. At .65 of a mile arrive at the concrete bridge spanning Wildcat Creek, from which the falls are viewed.

I found this low-volume waterfall most scenic during a late fall visit. Because of seeping water on its bedrock being frozen, the falls had the appearance of having more water than they actually did. (The 30'-wide rock face normally has only 5 to 10' occupied by flowing water.) Resembling a crystal staircase, ice covered two thirds of its rock face. The only open water flowed down its center. Eastern hemlock, hardwoods, and laurel flank the left side, with thick rhododendron to the right—its top is dotted with Fraser firs.

Brevard West

Cathey's Creek Falls

Roads: Graveled   A "5"
USGS Quadrangle: Rosman, NC
5 minutes, moderate, (no hiking map needed)

Note: Apply the following directions to the Brevard - Mt. Pisgah Area Map on pg. 88.

Directions: From the intersection of US 64 and US 276 *South*, in downtown Brevard, drive west on US 64 for 3.45 miles to Cathey's Creek Road (SR 1401, sign: Kuykendall Group Camp). Turn right (north) and in 50' turn left onto Selica Road (SR 1338). In 1.1 miles pass the Brevard water treatment plant, on the left. The road soon enters the Pisgah National Forest, where it is designated FS 471. After traveling approximately 2.5 miles, FS 471 switchbacks to climb King Mountain. Continue for a total of 3.2 miles to an easily-missed, single-vehicle pullout, on the right. (The power line crosses the road here.) Park and look carefully for a faint, bushwhacked path on the right.

Hike this descending path for 300' as it leads upstream to the base area.

Once there, carefully descend the bank to creek level, where the falls come into full view.

The upstream prelude to the falls may be seen from a bridge that crosses Cathey's Creek. To reach the bridge, continue north on 471 for approximately .1 of a mile.

Brevard - Mt. Pisgah Area

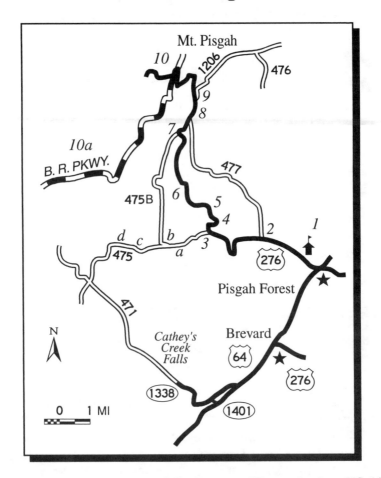

Directions: This route begins 3.5 miles east of Brevard, where US 64 and US 276 *North* intersect, near the community of Pisgah Forest. Drive north on US 276 to the following points of interest:

1. The Pisgah Ranger Station: 1.6 miles.
2. FS 477, access to the Twin Falls of Henry Branch: 2.3 miles.
3. FS 475, access to the falls in the Davidson River drainage: 5.4 miles. Take FS 475 the following distances to:
   3a. The State Fish Hatchery/Pisgah Center for Wildlife Education, access to the Falls on Cedar Rock and Grogan Creeks: 1.4 miles.
   3b. FS 475B, access to Slick Rock Falls: 1.5 miles.
   3c. FS 809, access to Cove Creek Falls: 3.25 miles.
   3d. FS 137, access to Jackson Falls: 3.95 miles.
4. Looking Glass Falls: 5.7 miles.
5. Parking and trailhead for Moore Cove Falls: 6.8 miles.
6. Sliding Rock: 8 miles.
7. FS 475B, access to the Falls on Log Hollow Branch: 10.5 miles.
8. The Cradle of Forestry in America/Forest Discovery Center: 11.35 miles.
9. FS 1206 (Yellow Gap Road), access to the High Falls on the South Fork, Mills River: 11.95 miles.
10. The intersection of US 276 and the Blue Ridge Parkway, south of Mt. Pisgah: 15.3 miles. Drive west on the parkway to:
    10a. The Graveyard Fields parking area, access to Yellowstone Falls: 7.1 miles.

1. The Pisgah Ranger Station (as above).

2. Twin Falls of Henry Branch

Roads: Graveled A "S" 60'	
USGS Quadrangle: Shining Rock, NC	
Trails (see text), 2.1 miles, water crossings, easy-moderate	

Directions: From US 276, take FS 477 for 2.6 miles to the Avery Creek parking area and trailhead, which is on the right.

Hike the descending, yellow- and blue-blazed Avery Creek Trail, which treads an old logging road. At .9 of a mile, in the creek bottom, arrive at a trail split and horse ford. The Lower Avery Creek Trail bends sharply right, while the route to the falls, the Avery Creek Trail, continues straight ahead. (This is a potentially confusing spot, as the hiking trail appears to cross Avery Creek at this ford. Instead, the trail meanders along the west creek bank, at times 7 or 8' above creek level, undulating its way to the Buckhorn Gap Trail.) At just over a mile, double blue blazes call attention to the intersection of the orange-blazed Buckhorn Gap Trail, which immediately crosses Avery Creek on a footbridge.

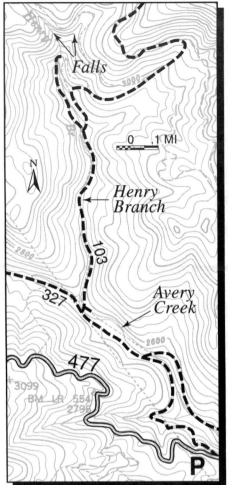

After crossing, enter an open area and look for double orange blazes and *possibly* a sign stating, "Buckhorn Gap." The trail abruptly turns left and initially treads an old logging railroad bed alongside Henry Branch. At 1.25 miles pass a potentially confusing horse ford. One-hundred ten feet upstream, the hiking trail crosses to the left side of Henry Branch on a footlog. Ascending the cove, the trail makes several other footlog crossings of Henry Branch. At just under 1.7 miles the hiking trail turns sharply left, while a horse ford continues straight ahead. Cross an unnamed creek here on steppingstones, 50' upstream from its confluence with Henry Branch, and tread a point of land between the two creeks. At 1.7 miles arrive at the blue-blazed Twin Falls Trail. (The Buckhorn Gap Trail continues straight ahead, up the point of land that separates the two creeks.)

The Twin Falls Trail veers left, at a 45° angle, and descends to cross a footlog. The Henry Branch cove soon widens and the trail once again ascends the *now* more discernible railroad grade. Two miles into the hike, dip to cross an unnamed branch, with a small, wet-weather waterfall up its cove (approximately 300' to the trail's left). Through the open woods of winter the Twin Falls soon come into view. The trail now becomes more difficult, as it climbs steeply. At 2.05 miles arrive at the Falls of Henry Branch (the first of the Twin Falls).

This waterfall has a large rock face to its right, and is broken into two major tiers. An open stand of poplar, straight and tall, populate its cove, along with hemlocks and banks of rhododendron that line the creek's upper reaches. The falls are best seen after rainfall. In the dry months they're little more than a thin, showering veil.

The falls up the right cove are less dramatic, falling 40' in several tiers. They are best seen from a point near the fire ring that precedes the first waterfall. This creek then cascades to its confluence with Henry Branch.

3. FS 475 (as above).

3a. Falls on Cedar Rock and Grogan Creeks

Roads: Paved   A "10" & A "4"
USGS Quadrangle: Shining Rock, NC, water crossing
Trail #'s 120 & 123, 25 minutes & 1 hour respectively, moderate

Directions: Cross the Davidson River and enter the fish hatchery/Pisgah Center parking area. Park at the Pisgah Center for Wildlife Education, which is .1 of a mile away.

From the southeast corner of the wildlife center, hike FS 475C due south. In 210′ pass the gate. Immediately cross a bridge spanning Cedar Rock Creek. In 100′ arrive at the Cat Gap Loop trailhead. (At the time of my hike a carsonite stake marked the trailhead.)

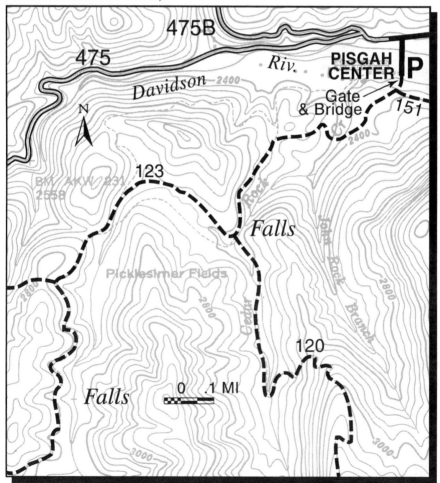

Entering the woods to the right, the orange-blazed trail initially ascends the foot of a ridge. At 600' the trail descends and bends slightly left. At the quarter mile cross a small creek. In another .1 of a mile cross Cedar Rock Creek on a footbridge that is designated as, "Robert's Bridge." Upon crossing the creek, the trail passes over a graveled road, crossing it diagonally (to the left). The trail now makes a 90° bend *right* to switchback up the mountainside, where it joins an old logging road (.4 of a mile). In this vicinity, through the open woods of winter, the impressive north face of John Rock may be seen to the southeast. The trail soon leaves the logging road and earshot of the creek as it enters a deep hollow. At .65 of a mile the trail arrives at and treads southwesterly on another logging road. Ascending at a moderate rate, the sounds of the creek soon return. At .85 of a mile look *for* and *take* a side path leading downhill to a primitive camping area adjacent to Cedar Rock Creek. An 8', shoaling waterfall lies just upstream.

To reach the lower falls, look downstream and take a path angling to the left (away from the creek) that gently descends the west side of the fall's cliff. At its base, turn back towards the creek and parallel the rock shelf for approximately 200' to the base of the falls.

This waterfall has some of the greenest, moss-covered rock that I've encountered. On a hot summer day pull up a rock and savor the natural air-conditioning as you enjoy its grace.

Return to the Cat Gap Loop Trail and continue upstream. In 200' intersect the blue-blazed Butter Gap Trail (#123). The Cat Gap Loop continues straight ahead, while the Butter Gap Trail (the route to the Falls on Grogan Creek) leads right, initially passing over a rock outcrop. Entering the Picklesimer Fields, closely encounter the oxbows of Grogan Creek. At 1.15 miles the trail intersects an old logging road then veers left to tread it. At 1.2 miles cross a small tributary branch. Soon thereafter (1.35 miles) intersect another logging road. In this area the trail is narrowed as it passes through hedge-like laurel thickets. (You'll get plenty wet passing through this thick growth after rain or snowfall.) One and forty-five hundredths miles into the hike, arrive at the orange-blazed Long Branch Trail.

The Butter Gap Trail continues to the left, outlining a couple of hollows, enroute to the Falls on Grogan Creek (1.9 miles). Upon arrival, scramble down the creek bank to observe the falls from their base.

3b. Slick Rock Falls

Roads: Graveled   A "3" 15', (no hiking map needed)
USGS Quadrangle: Shining Rock, NC
300', yellow blazed, easy

Note: Best seen after rainfall.

Directions: Turn right (north) onto FS 475B and drive 1.15 miles to the roadside parking area. The trail begins at the information board on the left side of the cove.

Winding and ascending, in 300' arrive at a side view of the falls.

3c. Cove Creek Falls

Roads: Graveled   A "5" 50'
USGS Quadrangle: Shining Rock, NC
Trail #361, 1.2 miles, 25 minutes, moderate

Note: Beware of the slick rocks in the pool area.

At this location you'll find the parking area on the left (south) side of FS 475. Park here. The route to the falls initially treads the gated FS 809 on the *north* side of FS 475. This road leads to the Cove Creek Group Campground and only campers are allowed to drive it.

From the gate, hike the graveled and ascending FS 809 (up Cove Creek). In 400' the road fords the creek, while the trail veers right to cross it on a footbridge. Road and trail soon rejoin. Four tenths of a mile up the road, just before arriving at the campground, look for the Caney Bottom Loop Trail on the left (west) side of the road.

The blue-blazed Caney Bottom Loop Trail initially parallels a small, unnamed creek and in 370' turns right to cross that creek (the Farlow Gap Trail [#106] splits, continuing straight ahead). A woodland trail, skirting the

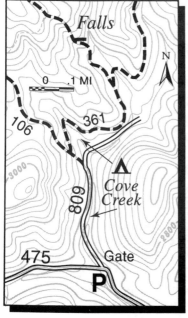

northwest side of the campground, at .55 of a mile pass through a small hollow and soon thereafter tread an old roadbed lined with laurel and rhododendron. With a long left bend, enter the hollow of Cove Creek. At .75 of a mile the blue-blazed Caney Bottom Loop Trail veers off to the right, while the unmarked fall's trail continues straight (double blue blazes call attention to this split, [there are occasional blue blazes further up the fall's trail]). Just shy of a mile, the trail passes through the depths of a hollow. Exiting this hollow, the falls now resonate through the woods. As the trail closely encounters Cove Creek (1.15 miles into the hike), arrive at the steeply descending side trail that leads downstream for .1 of a mile to the base of the falls. As you near the base, look for, then ponder the large out-of-place quartz boulder.

The fall's rock face is approximately 35' wide. Cove Creek clings to it in a foaming, sliding, whitewater flow. A shallow, gravel-filled pool extends 15 to 20' out from the base. Hemlocks are plentiful and rhododendron flanks its sides. Several hardwoods overhang the creek and frame the falls. A large jumble of boulders lie to the left side. The creek tumbles through rock, then is channeled between two large boulders. Splashing into another pool, the creek disappears into the downstream rhododendron.

3d. Jackson Falls

Roads: Graveled   A "5" 60'+
USGS Quadrangle: Shining Rock, NC
Trail #330 and woodland road, .45 of a mile, 10 minutes, easy-moderate

At this location you'll find a small parking area on the right. Park here. The hike begins at the gated road.

From the gate, the red-blazed Daniel Ridge Loop Trail treads the graveled FS 137. In 350' cross the Davidson River on a concrete bridge. Six-hundred fifty feet from the gate, the Daniel Ridge Loop leads left (straight) while FS

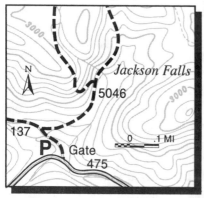

5046 (the route to the falls) veers right. Ascending and winding from this point, at .4 of a mile, the Daniel Ridge Loop reintersects 5046 from the left. The road-bed levels then descends and at .45 of a mile arrives at the base of Jackson Falls.

Sixty-feet high, with cascades below, this multitiered waterfall flows over a bold, blocky, rock face. Winter is my favorite time to visit. With the leaves off the sun works its magic on this south-facing cliff. Despite its easy access and great beauty, you'll find no crowds here.

4. Looking Glass Falls

Roads: Paved   A "10" 60', (no hiking map needed)
USGS Quadrangle: Shining Rock, NC, easy

This is possibly the most popular waterfall in the Brevard area. On summer days and during leaf season you'll have to jockey just to get a parking place. None the less, this is a great beauty with lots of water in all seasons. Being close to the highway, it is also a welcome relief when nursing blistered tootsies.

The falls may be seen from an overlook adjacent to the parking area. For a much better view take the stone stairway 150' down to creek level.

Despite being next to the highway, this is a very scenic spot with high rock walls and a large pool. The attraction has one *detraction*...LITTER! In spite of the fact that there are trash cans, unappreciative visitors can't seem to hit them. The Forest Service doesn't have the personnel to police the area, nor should they allocate manpower for that purpose, in the first place. If we are to pass these treasures on to our posterity, in their natural state, it's going to take self-government on all of our parts to see that they are not harmed.

5. Moore Cove Falls

Roads: Paved   A "5"
USGS Quadrangle: Shining Rock, NC
Trail #318, .7 of a mile, 20 minutes, easy-moderate

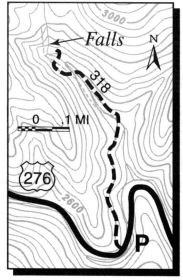

Note: Best seen after rainfall.

At this location there is a large parking area on the right shoulder of US 276. Park here. The trail begins at the northwest corner of the stone highway bridge that crosses Looking Glass Creek.

From the bridge, the yellow-blazed trail ascends, rounds the mountain's base, then descends back to creek level. The trail now starts its gradual climb up the cove, alongside Moore Cove Creek. At approximately .6 of a mile, the route steepens a bit as it rounds a bend to the right, whereupon the falls come into view.

This waterfall is very scenic, plunging an unbroken 60' from a massive, rock ledge. A pathway leads behind this thin, veil-like waterfall to a vantage point on the west side.

6. Sliding Rock (as above).

7. Falls on Log Hollow Branch

Roads: Graveled   A "4" 20'
USGS Quadrangle: Shining Rock, NC
.55 of a mile, easy

Directions: From US 276, turn left (south) onto FS 475B. Where the road makes a noticeable, hairpin bend to the left (1.65 miles) look for the pullout on the right. The hike treads the unmarked road located here and begins at the gate.

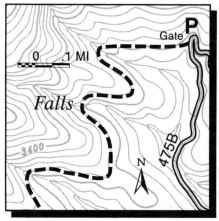

The roadbed is level at first, and in 390' enters a Forest Service refuse area. (Rock, pavement, and windfallen trees are stored here for further processing.) This also serves as a wildlife opening, as it is planted in grass. After passing straight through this opening, at 750', pass between wooden posts that once barricaded the road. The route to the falls is now gently undulating and somewhat curvy. At .2 of a mile cross a small creek on a rotting, one-lane auto bridge. (This, and another bridge further into the hike, are slick when wet and have holes large enough for a foot to slip through.) The roadbed bends sharply left, outlining this hollow, and at just over .3 of a mile, with Looking Glass Rock straight ahead in the distance, bends right to round a point of land (the sloping ridge line). Now entering the hollow of Log Hollow Branch, the road descends to the creek and the second, one-lane bridge (.55 of a mile). Cross the bridge and in 50' arrive at the side path to the falls. This pathway leads upstream approximately 50' to the viewing area.

Twenty-feet high, the creek flows out of the rhododendron then spills in cascades over a dark granitoid face. Towards the base, quartz mixes with and bands this dark rock.

8. The Cradle of Forestry in America/Forest Discovery Center (as above).

9. High Falls on the South Fork, Mills River

Roads: Graveled   A "4" 15'
USGS Quadrangle: Pisgah Forest, NC
Trail #133 and woodland pathway, 2 miles, water crossing (potentially deep and dangerous after periods of rain, see below*), moderate

Directions: From US 276, turn right (east) onto Yellow Gap Road (FS 1206) and drive 3.35 miles to Wolf Ford Road (FS 476, a.k.a. South Mills River Road). Turn right (south) and drive 1.35 miles to the parking area and gate.

Hike the South Mills River Trail (gated logging road). Initially, the trail descends at an easy rate beside the clear and fast-flowing South Fork of Mills River. At .65 of a mile look for a slim path leading 60' to river

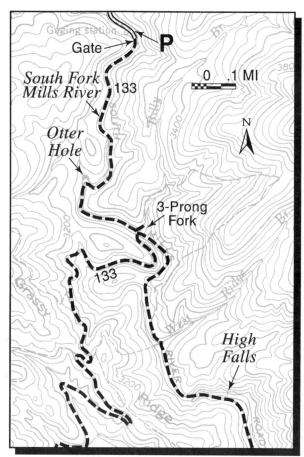

level and a landmark known as the Otter Hole. This beautiful pool is 70 to 80' in length and 60' wide.

Continuing downstream, the main trail now turns sharply left (southwesterly). In the vicinity of .85 of a mile pass a small fall, seen 15' below trail level. At .95 of a mile arrive at a three-prong fork. Two of the routes go to the left. The wider, South Mills River Trail goes to the right, leading to a concrete bridge 40' away.

Take the middle fork (that lies almost straight ahead) and in 50' cross Billy Branch on steppingstones. The fall's route status is now that of an unmaintained and unblazed woodland pathway. It is fairly rugged from here on: undulating over rocky and root-laced terrain with occasional windfalls. Immediately pass a fire ring to the path's left. After treading a tricky stretch (especially so when icy in winter) at 1.2 miles arrive at a high point of land where the pathway turns sharply left and descends. At 1.4 miles arrive back at river level amongst doghobble and galax. Soon thereafter (1.45 miles) cross West Ridge Branch. In a sharp left bend (1.55 miles) the path ascends to negotiate windfalls, then undulates back to river level. At 1.65 miles look for a fire ring approximately 30' to the left. Continuing, in just over 100' the path deadends into the river* where it is forced by impassable terrain to the opposite bank. There may be a large hemlock standing at this crossing. Shallow bedrock leads diagonally across the river here, and points the way into the rhododendron on its far side (N 80° E). After crossing, continue another .2 of a mile, on this often muddy stretch, to the fall's area.

10. The Blue Ridge Parkway (as above).

10a. Yellowstone Falls (Graveyard Fields Loop Trail) Mile 418.8, Blue Ridge Parkway, Haywood County, NC

Roads: Paved
USGS Quadrangle: Shining Rock, NC
Trail #358, moderate

Note: In late fall or early spring you may encounter icy trail conditions.

The area around Yellowstone Falls was scorched by fire in 1925 and again in 1942. The 1925 fire was started by sparks from a steam locomotive and consumed 35,000 acres of timberland. Left behind were charred tree trunks that resembled hundreds of headstones—thus the name, "Graveyard Fields."

The 1942 fire was caused by arson. Although there is plenty of vegetation

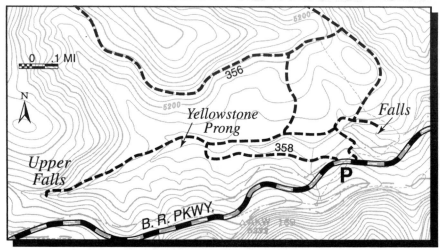

now, there are no large trees to speak of. For the most part the hillsides are covered in heath. Pin cherry thickets populate much of the flood plain. This pioneer tree (also known as fire cherry) is one of the first to colonize an area damaged by storms or fire.

The trail begins at the east end of the Graveyard Field's parking area. After descending wooden steps, this paved route winds through thick rhododendron. In 660' the pavement ends and the trail descends over rock and slightly rutted soil. At 795' exit the rhododendron and cross Yellowstone Prong on a double span, wooden footbridge. Now on the north side of the creek, the trail splits. The Middle Falls Trail leads right, while the Graveyard Fields Loop Trail/Upper Falls Loop Trail leads upstream.

Middle Falls

Hiking the winding trail downstream, in 125′ cross a small creek on steppingstones. At 420′ arrive at the top of the newly-constructed boardwalk. Descend this structure for approximately 400′ to the fall's viewing area.

Upper Falls

From the double bridge, the Graveyard Fields Loop Trail/Upper Falls Loop Trail initially treads the bedrock of Yellowstone Prong's north side (upstream). In 130′ the route leaves the creekbed and enters the heath. At 300′ the trail splits. Take the route on the left. At 740′ the trail exits the heath and turns upstream to follow the creek closely. At the quarter mile, the orange-blazed Graveyard Ridge Trail takes off to the north northeast. For the next .35 of a mile the Graveyard Fields Loop Trail/Upper Falls Loop Trail meanders up the flood plain, at times close to Yellowstone Prong, often not, to a point where it is intersected from the left by the return portion of the loop trail (.6 of a mile from the double bridge, see below**). The Upper Falls Trail spurs here and just past this intersection makes a brief turn north before continuing west. (The trail may be in the creek's overflow in several spots in this area.) Carrying this cumulative distance forth, at .7 of a mile cross a couple of small branches and enter a laurel thicket that has several Fraser firs in residence. At .9 of a mile cross a major tributary of Yellowstone Prong and soon thereafter a trickling tributary. One mile into the hike encounter the lower slopes of Black Balsam Knob, whereupon the trail begins its rocky and root-laced ascent of the Upper Fall's Cove. High up the cove, at 1.35 miles, arrive at a split. A path on the left leads to the creek, while the fall's trail makes an ascending right and left jog amongst the boulders. In 270′ arrive at the steppingstone viewing area of the Upper Falls.

In a cascading, whitewater flow, the creek occupies the right side of the 25′-wide bedrock exposure. Towards the base, the falls level into a foaming slide. During cold weather the shaded bedrock (on the creek's left side, at the base area) becomes ice covered. There is a great deal of rubble to the right side.

During a stormy, late fall visit, the falls seemed to meld with the sky, revealing their mystical origin, as dramatic gray and white clouds raced above them. The view of the Graveyard Fields (to the east) from the base area, was akin to a fine pastel painting. Beautiful, wind-swept clouds, with peeks of blue between them, allowed the sun to play on distant, straw-colored, rolling hillsides. Firs and large patches of red-brown heath stood out in stark contrast to these mute colors. I could make out Black Mtn. (east of Asheville) in the distance.

**Return Trail

Winding in "S" fashion, in 100′ cross the footbridge spanning Yellowstone Prong. In the floodplain, the trail then turns downstream. At approximately 500′ the route crosses several wet spots, via planks, then turns inland into the laurel and begins its ascent. At .45 of a mile arrive at the west end of a lengthy boardwalk. In just under .6 of a mile, arrive at the rock steps leading up to the parking area.

Saluda - Tryon Area

Pearson's Falls, Polk County, NC

Roads: Paved   A "10" 90'
Hours (3/1-10/31), open 10 a.m., close 6 p.m. Closed Mondays, except
holidays.
Winter hours (11/1-2/28), open 10 a.m., close 5 p.m. Closed Mon. and
Tues. Minimal fee, no entry 45 minutes before closing times.
.3 of a mile, easy, no hiking map needed

Though not on public lands, Pearson's Falls is one of the region's most popular destinations, receiving some 25,000 visitors a year. The falls and its glen are held and preserved by the Tryon Garden Club. The falls are named for their former owner, Charles William Pearson (Captain Pearson) who, while scouting a mountain route for the Asheville-Spartanburg Railway, now the Norfolk Southern, discovered them. In 1931, his son, in need of funds, was

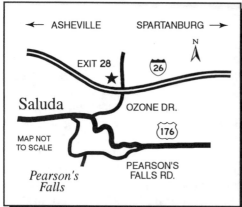

forced to sell a portion of his holdings. A planned sale to timber interests was averted when the Tryon Garden Club stepped in and purchased this unique natural area.

Directions: From Asheville, or Greenville/Spartanburg, via I-26, take Exit 28 (Ozone Drive). Drive south and in 1.2 miles intersect US 176. Turn left and travel 2.6 miles to Pearson's Falls Road (SR 1102). Turn right and drive .9 of a mile to the garden club entrance, which is on the left. Drive this access road for just over .1 of a mile to the parking area. The fall's trail begins at the apex of the cul-de-sac.

The trail ascends the Colt Creek drainage at an easy rate. In .2 of a mile pass the Frances Lightner ledge. This is a moss-covered, rock outcrop whose weeping shelves sustain brook lettuce and other water-loving plants. After crossing the creek via a stone bridge the trail continues another 400', terminating at the base of the falls.

Craggy Gardens Area

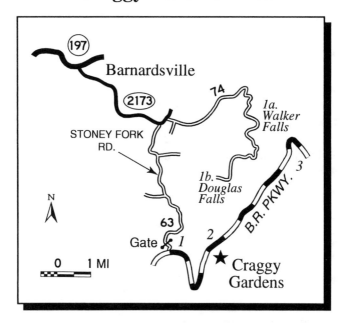

1. The Craggy Gardens Picnic Area: Mile 367.5 (approximate) Blue Ridge Parkway, access to (a) Walker and (b) Douglas Falls. Please note, this route may be gated where FS 63 intersects the picnic area access road. (See the text for alternate directions.)
2. The Craggy Gardens Visitor Center: Mile 364.6, Blue Ridge Parkway.
3. Glassmine Falls: Mile 361.2, Blue Ridge Parkway.

1(a) Walker and (b) Douglas Falls, Buncombe County, NC

Roads: High Clearance   Walker Falls A "1", Douglas Falls A "3"
USGS Quadrangles: Mt. Mitchell, Montreat, Craggy Pinnacle, NC
Easy

Both of these waterfalls are high on the north slope of Craggy Pinnacle and therefore don't flow heavily year-round. To see them at their best, visit after rainfall. That poses several problems though. FS 74's steep grades and long driving distance are trying enough when dry. Wet travel would make it even more so. Additionally, the freezing and thawing of winter would heave the road making spring travel rough.

Directions: (Please note, FS 63 may be gated at the picnic area access road.) From the Craggy Gardens Visitor Center, drive south on the Blue Ridge

Parkway for approximately 3 miles. Turn right onto the Craggy Gardens Picnic Area access road. In .3 of a mile turn left onto FS 63 (the road's designation changes to SR 2178 [Stoney Fork Road] upon entering private lands). Drive down this steep and winding graveled road and in 6.8 miles arrive at Dillingham Road (SR 2173). Turn right and drive 1.25 miles to a one-lane bridge* (see below).

Alternate directions: From I-40, in Asheville, drive north on US 19/23 for approximately 17.7 miles to NC 197 (the Barnardsville Exit). Turn right onto 197 and travel 6.2 miles, passing through the community of Barnardsville, while enroute to Dillingham Road (SR 2173). (The Barnardsville Volunteer Fire Dept. is located at the southwest corner of this intersection [just across the street from the post office].) Turn right and drive 5 miles to a one-lane bridge* (see below).

Walker Falls

*While crossing the aforementioned bridge, reset the odometer. The pavement gives way to gravel upon entering the Pisgah National Forest and the road's designation changes to FS 74. In .5 of a mile pass a road which intersects from the right. Drive approximately 4.3 miles to Walker Falls, which is on the left.

Walker Falls is a two-tier, sliding-type cascade with a total drop of 30'. Seen

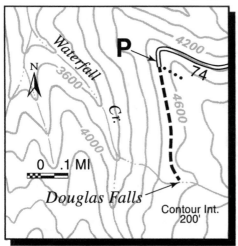

from the roadway, the creek enters the scene out of a hemlock-filled cove. Roadside briars and steep hillsides make an approach of the base not worth the effort. Spring, with its high water levels, offers the best viewing conditions.

Douglas Falls

To reach Douglas Falls, continue south on FS 74 for an additional 4.7 miles to the parking area at the road's end. Though the trailhead is not marked, it is easily located, being at the far end of the parking area and to the right. (There are several confusing pathways in the vicinity of the parking area.) The trail was well defined and easily discerned, despite the sparse blazes.

Spring arrives about a month later in this high country location than in the surrounding valleys. It is definitely cooler and the deciduous trees may lack the foliage of their lowland relatives.

The trail enters the woods heading due south and with an undulating rocky descent passes through a hardwood forest. In just over .3 of a mile cross a small, wet-weather branch and pass a massive, half-dead oak. It would take four people to reach around this ancient monarch. The trail now becomes a little tougher, undulating more than before, treading over rock and through several wet spots. At the half-mile point, the trail becomes somewhat easier as you escape the rock while passing through a stand of large hemlocks. Just ahead, while rounding a left bend, the falls come into view. Hike another 250' to the fall's viewing area.

Waterfall Creek clings to the rock face for 15' then lets go in a 40' sheer plunge, showering the rubble below. The cirque from which it falls is approximately 250 to 300' across with a 20' alcove behind the falls. Mosses and lichens adorn this massive bedrock exposure and rhododendron grows thick on its flanks. The creek exits the scene flowing through boulders littered with snagged tree trunks and woodland debris.

The cove's rich soil supports a huge colony of white violets and is dotted with their purple cousins. Buckeye and striped maple are abundant here. Downstream, the valley is filled with hemlock and some hardwoods. Atop the falls hemlocks reside along with the skeletons of their predecessors. Other wildflowers found here, include: corn flower, umbrella leaf, jack-in-the-pulpit, and several varieties of trillium.

The falls photograph best on an overcast day, or in the early morning before the sun peeks over the ridge from behind them.

2. The Craggy Gardens Visitor Center (as above).

3. Glassmine Falls, Mile 361.2, Blue Ridge Parkway, Buncombe County, NC

This ribbonlike, wet-weather waterfall may be seen from the parking area by looking due east across the gorge for a half mile, or so. A paved trail leads from the parking area, for 200', to an overlook where the falls are seen from a slightly higher vantage point.

I have visited this location on four separate occasions and only seen water on two of them (shortly after heavy spring rains). In summer and fall an appropriate name would be, "Bone Dry Falls."

Busick - Crabtree Meadows Area

1. NC 80 at Buck Creek Gap, access to (a) Roaring Fork Falls and (b) Setrock Creek Falls: Mile 344.1, Blue Ridge Parkway.

2. The Crabtree Meadows Campground and Visitor Center, access to Crabtree Falls: Mile 339.5, Blue Ridge Parkway.

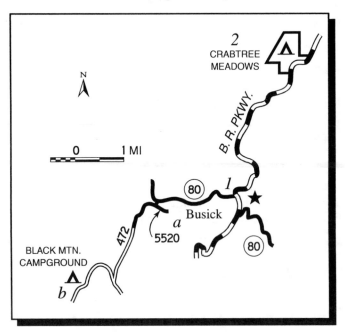

1a. Roaring Fork Falls, Yancey County, NC

Roads: Paved   A "10"
USGS Quadrangle: Celo, NC
.7 of a mile, easy

Roaring Fork is proof that a waterfall doesn't have to be big to be beautiful. More of a cascade than a waterfall, it spills five feet at a time over emerald-green, moss-covered rock ledges.

Directions: From the Blue Ridge Parkway and NC 80, drive west on NC 80. As you pass under the parkway begin your mileage check. In 2.2 miles, after passing through the community of Busick, arrive at FS 472*. Turn left, pass through the yield sign and cross Still Fork Creek on a small bridge. In less than .1 of a mile turn left onto FS 5520 (sign: "Busick Work Center"). Reset the odometer. Drive .15 of a mile and arrive at the work center. Park on the left shoulder, in the parking area provided, so as to not block the gates. Look for the gated road on the right (an unpaved continuation of FS 5520), which serves as the fall's trail.

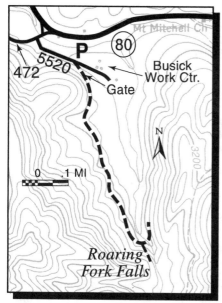

Hike uphill and in 730' pass a road that intersects from the right. At .25 of a mile pass the first of two concrete outbuildings. In .6 of a mile arrive at a culvert through which Roaring Fork flows. Look for the trail marker and trail on the right (west side of the creek). Hike upstream an additional 250' to the base area.

Roaring Fork is the region's most beautiful waterfall. It is housed in a deeply shaded cove of hardwoods and sparse hemlock. The multitiered cascade is approximately 40' high. The creek tumbles totally white in contrast to the dark green, moss-covered rock and rhododendron lining its banks. Look for a drill bit in the bedrock just up from the base of the falls. The bit secures a decaying sitting log in place for viewing the falls. A large, stratified boulder, to the right side of the viewing area, is decorated with lichens of all colors. After a more than 100' run down the mountain, Roaring Fork spills into a shallow, stone-filled pool whose waters have a light green tint.

*See Setrock Creek Falls.

1b. Setrock Creek Falls, Yancey County, NC

Roads: Graveled   A "5" 60'
USGS Quadrangles: Celo, Old Fort, NC in their margins
Mt. Mitchell and Setrock Creek Falls trails, .55 of a mile, easy

---

Note: This beautiful, wet-weather waterfall is easily reached via the Black Mountain Campground access road. Please park at the hiker's parking area, outside the campground's gate, unless you are using the camping facilities.

Directions: *See directions to Roaring Fork then proceed south on FS 472. In 1 mile the pavement ends. At 2.3 miles the road forks (in the vicinity of the now closed Neals Creek information station). At this fork turn sharply right and continue another .65 of a mile to trail parking, which is on the left.

The hike begins at the gate and bridge, 130' west of the parking area. I consider this the trailhead and distances will originate here. (For the first quarter-mile, the route to the falls and Mount Mitchell Trail are one in the same.)

From the gate, cross the South Toe River bridge and in 190' arrive at

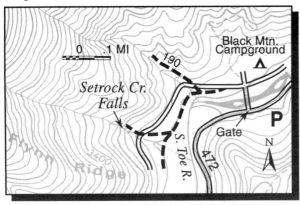

a crossroad. The campground's self-service pay station and host quarters are located here. At this location the route treads the road on the left, towards the Briar Bottom Group Camp. With another left, at just over .1 of a mile, the blue- and white-blazed trail leaves the roadbed. In 300' the trail makes a sharp right, while a path continues straight ahead. Making an oxbow, the trail closely encounters the roadbed once again. At the quarter-mile, the Mount Mitchell Trail (#190) splits off to the right (northwest), while the *now* unblazed route to the falls continues straight ahead (double blue blazes signify this split). After passing under a power line cross the rhododendron-obscured Little Mtn. Creek over a lengthy, wooden footbridge (.35 of a mile). In 180' arrive at the white-blazed Setrock Creek Falls Trail, which is on the right. (The bike path continues straight.) Narrowing slightly, in 215' (.4 of a mile) cross the service road and ascend steps as the trail reenters the woods. After a moderate ascent the trail levels and undulates over rock and roots while entering the cove of Setrock Creek. As you near the falls check out the fern-covered hillside. Another eye catcher is the overhanging trees from which the falls emerge.

2. Crabtree Falls Loop Trail,
Mile 339.5, Blue Ridge Parkway, Yancey County, NC

Roads: Paved   A "10" 60' Seasonal gas, food, and restrooms.
USGS Quadrangle: Celo, NC
Crabtree Falls Loop Trail, white blaze, .9 of a mile to falls
Full loop 2.6 miles, minor water crossings, moderate-difficult

Note: This trail is steep, rocky, and requires good ankle support.
Directions: From the Blue Ridge Parkway turn left (north) and drive .35 of a mile to the campground check-in kiosk. The parking area and trailhead are on the immediate right.

Enter the woods at the northeast corner of the parking lot and pass through a tunnel of rhododendron while descending at a moderate rate. In .15 of a mile the trail from the campground joins from the left. A wide depression, on the left, soon gives rise to a small branch. At just over .3 of a mile the trail makes a sharp right to head northeast. As the valley opens up to the left, you can hear

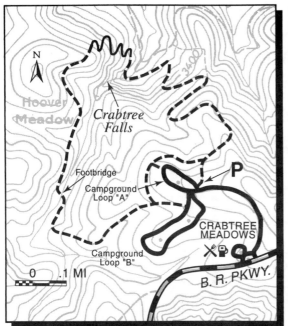

the rush of a creek far below. At .4 of a mile descend a flight of stairs. At their base the trail turns sharply left to head southwesterly. After descending two additional flights of stairs (.5 of a mile) the trail trends northeasterly. With a sharp left bend (.7 of a mile) head west. At .9 of a mile arrive at the fall's footbridge viewing area.

This captivating beauty adorns postcards and brochures found in shops up and down the parkway. Set in a heavily-shaded cove, Crabtree Falls is composed of hundreds of white water rivulets flowing down a black rock face. There is always ample water and scenery here. The falls are especially beautiful with spring's higher water levels. Its cove is littered with rubble ranging in size from 1' in diameter to that of a small car.

Leaving the falls, the trail initially heads downstream. The landmarks and highlights of the return portion of the loop are listed below.

- .9 to 1.1 miles: Ascending switchbacks.
- 1.15 miles: Top a rocky ridge line in the vicinity of the falls.
- 1.3 miles: Encounter Big Crabtree Creek.
- 1.4 miles: Boardwalk crossing of tributary branch.
- 1.45 miles: Cross boardwalk-type footbridge to east side of Big Crabtree Creek.
- 1.65 miles: Trail splits from creek.
- 1.75 miles: Encounter tributary to trail's right.
- 1.9 miles: Cross small, boggy tributary.
- 2.15 miles: Campground loop "B" access (right), 250' to campground.
- 2.4 miles: Campground access to falls leads straight ahead to tie into inbound portion of loop. Return portion of loop makes sharp right to head towards campground loop "A" and trail parking.
- 2.6 miles: Parking at trailhead.

Elk Park Area

Elk River Falls, Avery County, NC

Roads: Graveled   A "5" 30', Picnic area with fire grates
USGS Quadrangle: Elk Park, NC, TN
.2 of a mile, easy, (no hiking map needed)

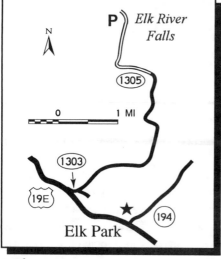

Note: Beware of the fast and deep waters of the plunge pool.

Directions: From the intersection of US 19E and NC 194, near Elk Park, NC, drive north on US 19E for 1.3 miles to SR 1303. Turn right and drive .25 of a mile to SR 1305 (a residential street). Turn left and zero your odometer. After driving 2.3 miles the pavement ends. Continue for a total of 4.1 miles to the parking area. The trail begins on its north end.

Hike .1 of a mile to a viewing area at the top of the falls. The best view, however, is at the base. To reach the base, continue downstream via steps which pass by a large, bedrock outcrop. In 300' arrive at the plunge pool.

The scenic Elk River pours over a wide and smooth rock face and into an immense plunge pool of unseen depths. Its waters are bounded and contained by bedrock and huge boulders.

"A-B" Linville Falls and Wilson Creek Area

Directions: From the intersection of US 221 and the Blue Ridge Parkway, north of the *community* of Linville Falls, drive north on the Blue Ridge Parkway to the following points of interest (parkway milepost locations are approximate). This area map is shared by routes A, B, C, and D.

A. The Blue Ridge Parkway Spur (Mile 316.4) access to Linville Falls: 1.1 miles.
B. NC 181 (Mile 312.1) access to Upper Creek Falls: 5.5 miles.
C. SR 1518 (Old Jonas Ridge Road, Mile 311.1) access to the falls in the Kawana and Lost Cove Area: 6.5 miles.
D. SR 1511 (Mile 307.9) access to the falls in the Roseboro and Mortimer Area: 9.75 miles.

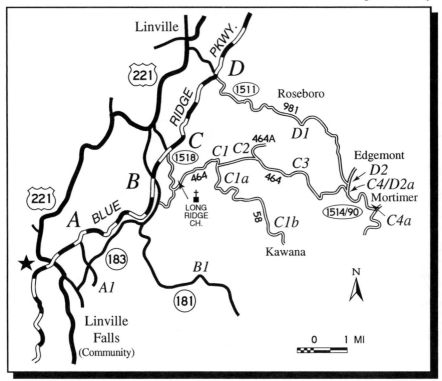

A1. Linville Falls,
Mile 316.4, Blue Ridge Parkway, Burke County, NC

Roads: Paved   A "10+" 15' & 45' respectively
Map: Linville Gorge Wilderness, or handout at visitor center
Easy to difficult, distances given are from the visitor center

This rugged and scenic gorge, with its beautiful waterfalls, is one of the Blue Ridge Parkway's main attractions, hosting thousands of visitors each year. You could spend a whole day here going from overlook to overlook drinking in the sights. In my opinion, the finest sight here is the Lower Falls when viewed from the base. If you can endure a difficult hike, I urge you to make this trek. Once in a lifetime memories await you there.

The river, gorge, and falls were named for explorer, William Linville, and his son, John, who died at the hands of local Indians. The Linville River was known to the Cherokee as, "Eeseeoh," which means, "a river of many cliffs."

Efforts to protect the area were made as early as the 1880's. All failed due to the lack of public funds. In 1950, John D. Rockefeller Jr. was persuaded of the area's importance by a photograph wielding Parkway Superintendent named, Sam Weems. Mr. Rockefeller donated $100,000 to purchase the falls and gorge for inclusion into the Blue Ridge Parkway. The gorge was given wilderness status in 1951, and was incorporated into the National Wilderness System in 1964. Today, some 10,975 acres are protected here.

Directions: Take the Blue Ridge Parkway Spur (south) for 1.4 miles to the parking area and visitor center. The trails originate here.

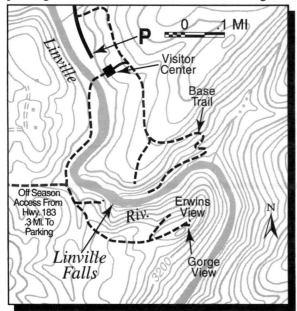

The scenic gorge offers hikes for all ages and abilities. For those *not acclimated* to hiking, I suggest the .5 of a mile (easy) hike to the Upper Falls and, if possible, the .7 of a mile (moderate) hike to Chimney View (the first overlook from which the Lower Falls are viewed). The other overlooks (described briefly, below) and base are rated from moderate to difficult.

Gorge View provides a vista of the mountains to the south and a brief glimpse of the Linville River far below.

Erwin's View affords a long-distance view (1500′ or more) of the Lower Falls and its plunge basin, as well as the spectacular gorge. Much of the area's beauty is owed to the Erwin quartzite walls flanking the river.

On the opposite side of the gorge is the .5 of a mile (moderate) hike to the Plunge Basin Overlook. Here you'll find a cliff-top perch offering a side view of the Lower Falls.

Plunge Basin Overlook and Base trails

From the visitor center, the trail to the base of Linville Falls climbs at a moderate rate for .25 of a mile then levels off. After hiking .35 of a mile arrive at the trail split. Straight ahead (or slightly right) is the side trail to Plunge Basin Overlook. There may be a sign here announcing, "Plunge Basin Overlook .2 of a mile, Linville Gorge .4 of a mile."

Level for the first .1 of a mile, the Plunge Basin Overlook side trail then descends at a moderate rate for the remaining .1 of a mile to the overlook.

To reach the basin itself, return to the main trail and continue hiking downstream.

Initially ascending, the trail soon begins its descent into the gorge. After passing through a split boulder arrive at the top of a flight of steps. At their base the trail treads over rubble and turns generally upstream while descending. From this point on, the trail is very rugged, rocky, and root laced. In the midst of giant hemlocks (.55 of a mile), pass beneath dazzling, moss- and lichen-covered Erwin quartzite cliffs. At .75 of a mile arrive at the river's edge. Hike upstream approximately 200' to the plunge pool viewing area. Narrow ledges and large boulders must be negotiated to reach the best vantage points. During periods of high water portions of this access may be submerged.

In May, Catawba rhododendron is in full bloom. Its purple-pink blooms enhance the beauty of the surroundings. Watch for heavy poison ivy growth amongst the alders in and around the rocky plunge pool area. The best time to photograph the falls (spring to fall) is between 10 a.m. and noon when they're fully front lit. On a blue-sky day this place is unbeatable!

Wilson Creek Area

The Wilson Creek Area holds some of the Blue Ridge Parkway's best kept secrets. The drive up the Wilson Creek drainage begins alongside a wide and slow moving creek flowing through private lands, and ends with fast running tributaries high on the slopes of Grandmother and Grandfather Mountains. Aside from having many beautiful creeks and waterfalls, the hardwood-covered mountainsides are also very scenic with rocky cliffs like the Big and Little Lost Cove Cliffs, which may be seen from the Blue Ridge Parkway.

The Wilson Creek Trail System was developed to take pressure off the heavily used Shining Rock Wilderness. It seems that Wilson Creek hasn't caught on. If you're looking for a remote locale with plenty of scenery, you've just found it.

In spring, wildflowers such as crested dwarf iris, firepink, jack-in-the-pulpit, violet, and at least three varieties of trillium are found along many of the area's trails. In May, Catawba rhododendron is in bloom followed by the laurels which bloom in June. Trees native to the area, include: oak, hickory, maple, beech, American holly, hemlock, white pine, and Fraser magnolia.

The Wilson Creek Area has many trophy trout streams and is a haven for wildlife—deer, turkey, and black bear call the region home. Streamside, the spotted sandpiper may be seen hopping from rock to rock searching for food, comically bobbing all-the-while.

South of the Upper Creek Fall's parking area, on NC 181, is the Brown Mountain Overlook, where it is said that the Brown Mountain Lights shimmer on nights when conditions are right. According to local folklore, the lights shine from a slave's lantern as he looks for his lost master.

Near the community of Mortimer, the walls of an old mill stand in ruin. The mill was destroyed by a flood, in 1940. What astounds me, is that the area had any commerce that long ago—it's that remote.

These ruins and the barren bedrock seen along many of the area's creeks, are testament to the power of flash floods.

B1. Upper Creek Falls Loop Trail, Burke County, NC

Roads: Paved   A "10" 30' with shoals below
USGS Quadrangle: Chestnut Mtn., NC
Trail #268B, orange blazed, full loop 1.6 miles, short route .5 of a mile,
water crossings,   moderate-difficult

In my opinion this is the most scenic waterfall in the Wilson Creek Area.

Directions: From the Blue Ridge Parkway, take NC 181 south for approximately 6 miles. The Upper Creek Fall's parking area is on the left (adjacent to the 22 MP on NC 181). The hike can be made from either the east or west side of the parking area. The short route to the falls begins on the west side of the parking area. (Directions for the short route are given in italics below.)

Loop Trail

Hiking the loop in a counterclockwise direction, head east. The trail (which is unblazed on this leg) immediately enters an open field and veers sharply left. The trail now descends the rubble of road construction via steps and switchbacks. While descending, the switchbacks progressively lengthen. At times the trail undulates, passing by and over large rocks. At .55 of a mile the falls may be heard through the woods. At .8 of a mile the trail makes a sharp left then meanders between and beneath large boulders, the most notable of which juts some 40' into the air. The trail soon makes another sharp left and continues descending. At .85 of a mile arrive at Upper Creek. Just upstream lies a 10'-high, chute-type waterfall with shoaling cascades below.

The creek flows through a large bedrock exposure, with streamside rhododendron on the left, and barren rock on the right. Looking downstream, the creek runs for approximately 100 yards over barren rock and disappears into the valley. (A very beautiful area.)

The trail crosses Upper Creek (a rather l-o-n-g jump's width) just below the lower falls. After negotiating the steep bank continue upstream. The trail then climbs steeply and passes through a rocky area (.95 of a mile). At 1 mile look for a pathway that leads to the lower viewing area of Upper Creek Falls.

Descend this pathway to a small, rocky, beach-like area with a pool sporting large, Erwin quartzite boulders that are crisscross banded with white quartz. These boulders must be negotiated to view the falls, which lie just upstream.

Return to the main trail and continue upstream. The side view of Upper Creek Falls lies just ahead (1.05 miles). The trail then switchbacks up the mountainside to circumvent the fall's cliff. At 1.25 miles pass through a primitive campsite then descend to the creekside just above the falls. Hemlock and fir are in abundance in this magnificent setting.

Upon arriving creekside, look upstream for a small, shoaling-type waterfall

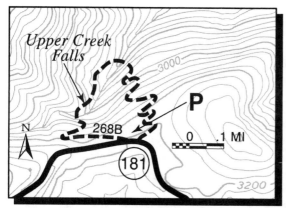

in the distance. Upper Creek then rushes through a maze of large boulders and out onto slick rock before spilling into the valley below. Most noteworthy from this vantage point is the fine view of Cold Mountain and Simmons Ridge to the north and Sugar Knob to the northeast.

Carefully boulder hop the creek. The *now* orange-blazed trail switchbacks steeply uphill and soon parallels NC 181 enroute to the parking area .4 of a mile away.

Short Route to Falls

Upon entering the woods, the orange-blazed trail ascends for .1 of a mile while paralleling NC 181. The falls are heard in this area. At .2 of a mile, the trail switchbacks steeply downhill on its way to the top of the falls, which are another .2 of a mile away.

To reach the base area, look for the trail entering the laurel on the north side of Upper Creek. (Directly across from where you exited the woods when you arrived at creek level.) Boulder hop the creek and pass through a primitive campsite. The trail now switchbacks down the steep mountainside. In .2 of a mile notice an opening where the falls are viewed from the side.

From this point the main trail descends to the base area another 300' away. Descend a short side path to a rocky, beach-like area. The distant falls may be seen from large boulders that litter the creekbed here.

"C" Kawana and Lost Cove Area

C. Directions: From the Blue Ridge Parkway, take SR 1518 (Old Jonas Ridge Road, a graveled road) for 1.75 miles to the Long Ridge Baptist Church. FS 464 is straight ahead. Check your mileage from the church and take FS 464 to access the following points of interest:

C1. FS 58, access to (a) North Harper Creek Falls and (b) South Harper Creek Falls: 2.55 miles.

C2. FS 464A, access to the Falls on Little Lost Cove Creek: 4.1 miles.

C3. The parking area and trailhead for Hunt Fish Falls: 6.35 miles.

C4. The intersection of SR 1514/90, south of Edgemont: 9.5 miles. (Same as location D2a. on the Roseboro and Mortimer Area route.) Take SR 1514/90 south to:

   C4a. The Mortimer Work Center, access to the Falls on Thorps Creek: 1.8 miles.

C1. The intersection of FS 58 (as above).

C1a. North Harper Creek Falls, Avery County, NC

Roads: Graveled   An "8" 25'
USGS Quadrangle: Chestnut Mtn., NC
Trail #266, 1 mile, water crossings, moderate-difficult

Directions: From the intersection of Forest Service roads 58 and 464, drive south on FS 58 for .25 of a mile. Look for the parking area and trailhead on the left. Park here. The North Harper Creek Trail enters the woods at the south end of the parking area.

Descending inground steps, in 45' the trail turns sharply left to follow a small branch downstream. Descending still further, at 250' the trail turns right and soon crosses this branch. Next, pass by a confusing pathway on the left which leads to a campsite. Meandering, at .1 of a mile, pass red painted trees which denote the boundary of Forest Service land and private property. The rushing sounds of North Harper Creek soon break the silence. At .2 of a mile the trail descends to cross North Harper Creek on steppingstones. On its east side the trail continues down the creek's bedrock and reenters the woods. At the quarter mile encounter a large bedrock exposure with the creek some 30' away. The trail turns left and again reenters the woods. Just ahead, after passing through laurel, again tread exposed bedrock with a private residence off to the left. (On account of seeping water this rock may be slick with algae or icy in winter.) Once again the trail reenters the woods. On the steep slope for the next 1200', the trail treads rubble-like rock amongst boulders, and crosses wet spots and wet-weather branches. At the half-mile point pass through a jumble of fallen trees. After crossing another wet-weather branch (.6 of a mile) the trail turns right and descends towards North Harper Creek. Cross to the south side of the creek over large boulders. The trail then passes through a rhododendron thicket and a group of boulders while winding its way along the creek's flood plain enroute to the next crossing. At .7 of a mile cross to the north side of North Harper Creek. The trail soon exits the rhododendron for open woods and at .75 of a mile passes a fire ring. In 40' Trail #238 intersects on the left, while the North Harper Creek Trail (the fall's trail) continues right. At .8 of a mile arrive at a fire ring atop the falls.

The creek makes a 400'-long uneven slide, over a broad and rugged expanse of bedrock, before flowing over the edge. Seen to the southeast from this vantage point is the distant Simmons Ridge. At the top of the slide, look carefully for the trail to the base which continues across the creek.

With two leaps, hop the creek (whose flow is split in half by bedrock). Reenter the woods and continue downstream. The trail is more easily hiked on

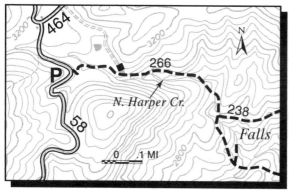

this (the south) side of the creek as the terrain is not as rocky and the grades are constant. At .9 of a mile the North Harper Creek Trail continues straight ahead while the base trail departs with a sharp left. The base trail descends more steeply (.95 of a mile) as the sound of falling water becomes evident. Enter the streamside rhododendron and meander towards the creek whereupon the falls come into full view. After hiking 1 mile arrive at their base.

This beautiful waterfall slides over an iridescent gray bedrock formation that is smooth and rounded at the top. The bedrock exposure is approximately 80' wide with the creek occupying 6' of its width at the top, fanning out to 8-10' at the base. The majority of its waters cling to the bedrock in a steep slide. When the creek is up, a portion of its waters become airborne in roostertail fashion. Algaes grow in the flowway and rock tripe has colonized the sun-baked bedrock on its sides. The creek slips into a small pool which is dammed by a large bedrock exposure. Running 40', from left to right, this bedrock dams the pool's extreme left side. Flowing out of the pool's right side, the creek encircles a small island then exits the scene over beautiful boulders. Birch, alder, hemlock and poplar populate the island.

The falls photograph best either in the early morning or late afternoon when full sunlight is absent. An overcast day also works well.

C1b. South Harper Creek Falls, Avery County, NC

Roads: Graveled/High Clearance   A "10"
USGS Quadrangle: Chestnut Mtn., NC
Trail #260, 1.5 miles, potentially deep water crossing at falls, moderate-difficult

Note: After driving 2.6 miles, FS 58 gets pretty rough. It can be driven, if careful, in an automobile with good clearance.

Directions: Drive south on FS 58 for a total of 4.3 miles to the parking area which is on the right (or north side of FS 58 on account of the way the road bends). The trail begins on its south side.

The trail enters the woods passing through a laurel thicket and mixed hardwoods. In 100' the trail bends left to enter a windfall-strewn hollow while descending. Out of the hollow's depths, at .1 of a mile, the trail ascends while

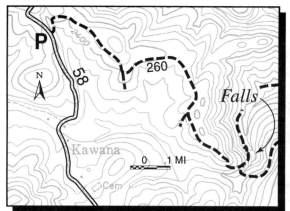

heading in a southerly direction. At 800' the trail starts descending and soon bends left. Bottoming out at the quarter mile, ascend to tread atop a saddle. Leaving the high point of the saddle, at just over .3 of a mile, the route turns southerly to avoid a knob that lies dead ahead. At .55 of a mile the trail turns sharply left (east). (A path on the right, at this location, leads due south to private land.) After passing over a ridge line enter the high end of an open woodland hollow, first turning northerly, then to the east. In the area around .75 of a mile tread the crest of the ridge while heading southeasterly. At 1.05 miles look for another path, on the right, leading to private property. Stay left here. The South Harper Trail continues south and at 1.15 miles arrives at the first group of red painted, bearing trees. Views of the isolated community of Kawana are present at this location. The trail turns southeasterly and soon begins a noticeable descent along the crest of a ridge. As the descent steepens (1.3 miles) pass more bearing trees and a survey marker. (South Harper Creek may be heard in this area.) In switchback fashion the trail bends right, then left, and at 1.45 miles, within sight of the creek, arrives at the junction of the Raider Camp Trail (#277), which leads right. The trail to the falls leads left (downstream). In 135' arrive in the vicinity of the top of the falls. The trail soon starts a very steep descent into the fall's cove. Two switchbacks lie ahead. As you exit the *second* switchback find yourself in the proximity of the *now* inaccessible base of the falls. Pace off 200' while heading downstream, then look for the gully that allows access to creek level. This rocky access leads 50' down to the creek. Once there, rock hop or wade the creek. The falls are seen approximately 200' upstream.

The massive bedrock exposure that houses the falls is shaped like a flared cone, with one side missing. (That side being to the northwest, from which the creek flows.) The smooth walls are very beautiful and streaked with colorful, mineral varnishes. In May, Catawba rhododendron blooms on its forested rim. Where humus-filled fissures allow, sparse trees grow out of its 120'-high walls. This bright white waterfall slides for 100' over bedrock and slips into a small, boulder-filled pool.

C2. Falls on Little Lost Cove Creek, Avery County, NC

Roads: Graveled/High Clearance   Upper A "6" Lower A "4"
USGS Quadrangle: Grandfather Mtn., NC
No official trail, 1.5 miles, minor water crossings, difficult

---

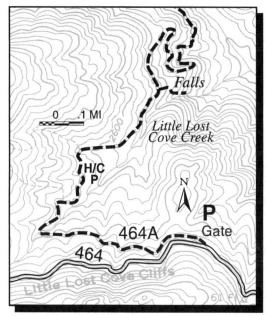

Note: Periodically, the gate may be open allowing you to drive FS 464A to the primitive campsite mentioned below. Driving my high-clearance truck, I cringed at every high spot in the road, hoping that I wouldn't bottom out.

For the benefit of those who do not have high-clearance vehicles, hiking distances are given from the gate. If you are able to drive to the high-clearance parking area, mentioned below, subtract .9 of a mile from the applicable distances given.

At this location park at the gate.

Hike (or drive) the descending and undulating FS 464A. In .65 of a mile the road crosses Little Lost Cove Creek. At .9 of a mile pass a large opening (primitive campsite/high-clearance parking area) on the right.

Continuing from the campsite, in 70' pass by several large, jeep-blocking mounds. Cross a creek at 215', whereupon the roadbed turns northeasterly. The old roadbed then meanders in a northerly direction while descending to cross another creek at 575'. (In flood, this creek overflows its culvert and washes the road, exposing lots of ankle-twisting rock.) After this crossing, the roadbed descends at a more moderate rate while heading due east. At 1.15 miles the road turns more northeasterly and the sounds of Little Lost Cove Creek are now heard through the woods. After hiking a total of 1.45 miles look very carefully for a path, on the right, bushwhacked into the rhododendron. (This path leaves 464A at a 90° angle and leads to the base of the falls.)

The pathway descends rather steeply into the thicket, and in 70' turns south. After winding down the steep slope, at 1.5 miles intersect the upper extremities of an old roadbed (which now serves as the path) alongside the upper falls. To view them from the base, descend the galax-covered bank and cross the creek (a large boulder hides their view from the roadbed).

Located in a cool, heavily shaded cove, the two-tier upper falls are approximately 40' high. Its upper tier is almost totally hidden from view. The lower tier falls 20' over the right side of the 60'-wide rock face. Four-feet wide at the top, the flow fans out to 8 to 10'. The creek is dammed by a large boulder near the base which forces its waters to the left. The cove is filled with small hardwoods. Lesser amounts of rhododendron are found on either side of the falls. Where shaded, the rock is green with mosses—where exposed to the sun rock tripe thrives. The best photo vantage point is to the left side of the falls which is easily reached via three large boulders.

The clear, sandy-bottomed creek flows, disappearing into the woods, on its way to the lower, shoaling falls.

To reach the base of the lower falls, return to the path (overgrown logging road) and hike downstream for 600'.

Lower Little Lost Cove is a 60' slide over a 50'-wide bedrock face. The slide is split at the top, with 2' of its flow on the left, and 5' on the right. These waters commingle into a 15'-wide sliding flow that lands among boulders. The creek then cascades into a small pool that lies 100' downstream from the base of the falls. Dammed by a large boulder, the creek is easily crossed for better viewing.

C3. Hunt Fish Falls, Avery County, NC

Roads: Graveled   A "2" 8' two tiers
USGS Quadrangle: Grandfather Mtn., NC
Trail #263, .9 of a mile,   minor water crossings,   moderate-difficult

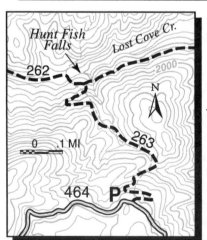

At this location look for the trailhead on the east side of the parking lot.

The trail enters the hardwood forest and descends at a moderate rate while meandering in switchback fashion. In just over .1 of a mile pass through a rhododendron thicket with hardwoods interspersed. At .3 of a mile tread a ridge line between two hollows. (The view to the east, in this vicinity, is very nice when the leaves are off.) With a knob lying dead ahead, the trail turns sharply left as it enters the high end of a hollow. Now treading the right (east) side of this north-opening hollow, the trail soon parallels a small branch that rises within it. At .55 of a mile cross to the left side of this branch. In 400' cross another branch (on steppingstones) just above their creek-forming juncture. Sixty-five hundredths of a mile into the hike, the trail veers left and away from the creek to switchback down the hillside (at a moderate rate). At .85 of a mile arrive at the junction of the Lost Cove Creek Trail (#262). Hike downstream (east) for just over 200' and cross the tributary creek (that accompanied us on much of the hike) as you exit the woods.

This creek has a set of wet-weather falls (seen to the right). They are slim and drop a total of 40'. This unnamed creek joins Little Lost Cove Creek at Hunt Fish Falls. In fact, the exposed bedrock just downstream from its falls provides the viewing area for Hunt Fish Falls.

Hunt Fish Falls is a 15'-wide uniform curtain of water that falls approximately 8' into a bedrock-contained pool. The creek is then channeled to the right through a flume and makes a sliding entry into a V-shaped pool of considerable size and depth. The bedrock from which the falls are viewed has water-filled potholes that teem with tadpoles in the springtime. The creeks in the Wilson Creek area rage in flash flood and leave large expanses of barren rock in their wake. The bedrock exposed at Hunt Fish Falls is of the Plutonic variety. This is a beautiful spot with adequate foliage as a backdrop.

C4. SR 1514/90 (as above). Also see D2a. Roseboro and Mortimer Area.

C4a. Falls on Thorps Creek, Caldwell County, NC

Roads: Graveled A "4" 12'
USGS Quadrangle: Chestnut Mtn., NC, US fee campground
Trail #279, .2 of a mile, minor water crossing, easy, picnic facilities

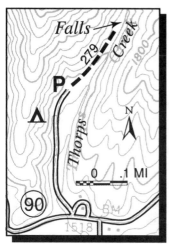

Directions: From the entrance to the Mortimer Campground and SR 90, drive the campground road for .3 of a mile to its apex (loop road) and park. The trail begins here.

The trailhead is not marked and the trail has no blazes, but the route generally follows Thorps Creek *upstream* at a distance of 50 to 60'. After hiking just under .2 of a mile arrive at the base of this small but very ornate waterfall.

Thorps Creek falls 4' over moss-covered rock, then slides 8' into a small and shallow, bedrock-lined pool. Large beech and white pines stand amongst the surrounding rhododendron. Other plants include, American holly and Solomon's seal.

Be very careful while jockeying for a frontal view. The bedrock in front of the falls appears deceptively safe. In reality, it's a slick and treacherous bun buster.

Please haul out the trash that unappreciative visitors have hauled in.

"D" Roseboro and Mortimer Area

D. Directions: From the Blue Ridge Parkway, take SR 1511/FS 981 (Roseboro Road, a graveled road) to the following points of interest:

D1. The concrete bridge spanning Gragg Prong, access to the Falls on Gragg Prong: 4.8 miles.

D2. The intersection of SR 1514/90 at the community of Edgemont: approximately 9.25 miles. From this intersection, drive south on SR 90 the following distance to:

D2a. The intersection of FS 464: .2 of a mile. (Same as location C4, Kawana and Lost Cove Area.)

D1. Falls on Gragg Prong, Avery County, NC

Roads: Graveled   A "6"
USGS Quadrangle: Grandfather Mtn., NC
Trail #262, 1.5 miles, water crossings, moderate

Directions: Just prior to crossing the concrete bridge at this location, look for a dirt road (on the west side of the bridge) that parallels Gragg Prong downstream. Drive this road for 200', to its end and park. The trail begins creekside at the tree line. Look for the white blazes that denote the trail.

Note: If the bedrock encountered at the beginning of this hike is anywhere close to being submerged *do not hike this trail.* The creek would be far too deep to be safely forded downstream.

Entering the woods the trail crosses a small, unnamed creek flowing off Timber Ridge. Treading a rocky stretch, the trail soon passes alongside Gragg Prong then turns uphill through a tunnel of rhododendron. After undulating some 15 to 30' above creek level, at the quarter mile the trail descends and momentarily loses sight of Gragg Prong. At .3 of a mile arrive back at creek level. Undulating once again, at .4 of a mile the trail arrives at creek level and the first major water crossing. In the vicinity of a small island, look for a suitable crossing. On the left (east) side of the creek (.45 of a mile) look for a small opening with a side path leading down to the creek's water-sculpted bedrock. Return to the main trail which now passes through laurel and

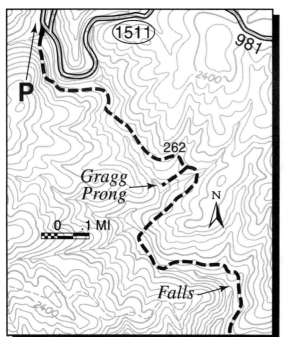

rhododendron on a much better treadway.

At .65 of a mile the trail ascends slightly and leaves sight of the creek as it heads inland. In this southeast bend reach a high point (.7 of a mile) and descend to enter a hollow. Dense, hedge-like laurel and rhododendron line the trail in this vicinity. At just over .75 of a mile note a side trail leading downstream alongside a tributary branch. *This will be explored later (see below).

The main trail continues into the hollow and dips to cross its branch on steppingstones. Now ascending, round a left bend as you top a small ridge. The trail then descends to cross another small tributary at .8 of a mile. Out of its hollow the trail heads southwesterly and with a gradual bend turns south. Nine tenths of a mile into the hike, look for a 15' side path leading to a high point where the creek may be observed, far below, running through its V-shaped, rock gorge. (Be extra careful at this unprotected exposure, there's a 40' drop.)

The trail now turns downhill and at the one-mile point arrives back at creek level. After a long left bend the trail crosses Gragg Prong (1.05 miles). Tread the waters of a small tributary for 30' and reenter the woods. After passing a jutting boulder outcrop, on the trail's left, cross a small tributary branch. At 1.15 miles look for a suitable crossing to the east side of Gragg Prong. The trail now ascends and at 1.2 miles arrives at a spot with exposed bedrock and deep pools. Treading bedrock alongside the cascading creek, the trail reenters the woods. (Because of the cascade's descent, the trail is now high above the creek.) At 1.25 miles pass a slim pathway that leads to a stoney beach area. Generally descending, in an undulating manner, after crossing the *second* of two small tributaries (just over 1.45 miles) look *for* and *take* the short side path to top of the falls.

While the falls on Gragg Prong are not the most impressive, the setting is. The 200'-long falls slide over a wide bedrock exposure and into a very rugged gorge. Downstream, boulders have tumbled into the gorge while others teeter awaiting their turn. Provided there is enough water, this is a great spot for waterfall/autumn leaf shots. Alders grow out of its fissured rock.

*This side trail leads 300' to a camping spot with a stoney and sandy beach-like area. Beautiful boulders and some very interesting, tilted bedrock are exposed here. In the creek's overflow area the bedrock is potholed. A small waterfall lies upstream. Its waters carve out a deep pool and are undermining bedrock on the creek's west side.

D2. SR 1514/90 (as above).

D2a. FS 464 (as above).

Blowing Rock Area
Mile 294.5, Blue Ridge Parkway

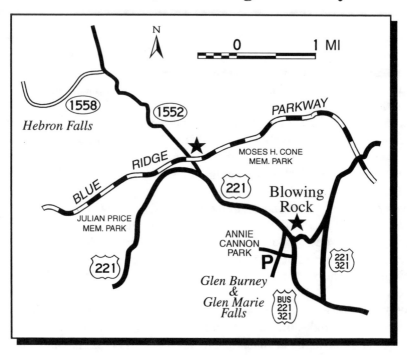

Hebron Falls, Watauga County, NC

Roads: Graveled   A "5"
USGS Quadrangle: Boone, NC
.5 of a mile, 20 minutes, water crossings, easy-moderate

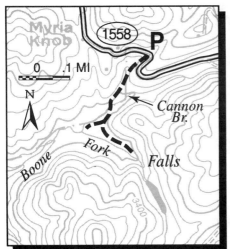

Note: This waterfall is very different from others in the area. The cove below the falls is littered with scores of massive boulders. To fully view the falls, you'll have to do some tricky boulder hopping.

Directions: From the Blue Ridge Parkway, north of Blowing Rock, take the US 221 (Flannery Fork—Shull's Mill Road) exit. Where the exit splits, veer right, then turn right (north) onto Shull's Mill Road (SR 1552). Zero your odometer while passing under the Blue Ridge Parkway overpass. In 2 miles arrive at Old Turnpike Road (SR 1558). Turn left. Drive 1.35 miles and look for a pullout on the right. (The road bends sharply left here.) Park here. (If you pass the "Grace Home" you've gone too far.) The unmarked trail is directly across the road from the pullout.

From the parking area, the trail leads downhill on an old logging road that parallels the left side of a small, unnamed branch. In .2 of a mile cross this branch. Shortly thereafter, the unnamed branch joins Cannon Branch and the trail makes a shallow crossing below their confluence. Now following Cannon Branch downstream, in another .1 of a mile (.3 of a mile into the hike) the trail forks left at a large rock to parallel Boone Fork upstream. (Traveling up Boone Fork is rather difficult, as the trail is forced onto the rubble-like boulders in the creek itself, by impassable laurel thickets and a small cliff [encountered 150' from the aforementioned rock]). A portion of the falls can be seen as you arrive at the creek bank. For a full view, however, you'll need to do some boulder hopping. Continue upstream 800' to view the falls.

Glen Burney and Glen Marie Falls, Watauga and Caldwell Counties, NC

Roads: Paved   A "5" & A "6" respectively
USGS Quadrangles: Globe, Boone, NC, in their margins
1.2 miles,   minor water crossings,   difficult

Directions: From the intersection of US 221 and Bus. 321, in Blowing Rock, drive south on Bus. 321 (Main St.) for .15 of a mile to Laurel Lane. Turn right and drive .1 of a mile. After crossing Wallingford St., look for the Annie L. Cannon Memorial Park, on the left. Park here. The trail begins at the southwest corner of the parking lot.

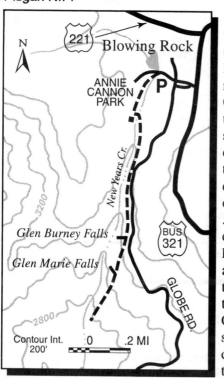

221 Blowing Rock

N

ANNIE
CANNON
PARK

P

New Years Cr.

3200

Glen Burney Falls

BUS
321

Glen Marie Falls

GLOBE RD.

2800

Contour Int.   0   .2 MI
200'

Initially treading an old service road, in 115', in sight of a pump station (which lies straight ahead), the trail leaves the roadbed. Turning sharply right, descend to cross New Years Creek on steppingstones (180'). The trail now turns left to follow the west side of the creek. In the vicinity of a concrete block structure, the trail treads level while passing private property, which lies to the left side of the creek and the right side of the trail. At .2 of a mile the trail encounters rhododendron and becomes more woodland oriented. At .3 of a mile pass by a confusing side path, on the left. The trail now descends while bending right then switchbacks into the New Year's Creek bottom. While passing an old sewage treatment plant, whose concrete foundation lies to the right, the trail turns sharply right, near creek level, then meanders downstream. The rhododendron-lined trail now more closely follows New Years Creek downstream. At .45 of a mile pass a steppingstone creek crossing which leads to private property. The Glen Burney Trail turns right here and ascends to circumvent thick, streamside rhododendron then arrives back at creek level to cross a footbridge over New Years Creek. On the creek's east side, ascend steps and tread an old logging road. At .55 of a mile arrive at a rocky, rough spot and a close encounter with Globe Road. (People have dumped an assortment of litter from the road onto the hillside, here.) The trail now descends at a more moderate rate. Seven tenths of a mile into the hike, arrive at the top of a waterfall known as, "The Cascades."

A wooden bridge atop this cascade offers views, both up and downstream. Downstream from the bridge, is a sliding-type waterfall with a 40' run and a drop of 20'. In the spring, while looking downstream to the creek's left side, you may see an almost magenta-colored variety of large-flowered trillium covering the creek bank. Return to the main trail and continue downstream.

After descending steps the trail undulates 15 to 20' above the creek, then begins its rocky descent once again. The New Year's Creek gorge now widens and the trail turns away from the creek. At .85 of a mile arrive *at* and *take* a 100' side trail to the top of Glen Burney Falls.

From the observation deck looking upstream, the cascade enters the scene in reverse "S" fashion. The creek then flows by the deck and makes a 40' shoaling slide over bedrock, disappearing over the edge of the abyss.

From the top of Glen Burney, the main trail turns away from the creek as the gorge further widens. At .95 of a mile the trail turns right, and via a switchback, descends. (A side path, on the left, at this location leads uphill to private property.) At the base of the first switchback (just over 1 mile) look *for* and *take* a rocky side trail leading upstream for 325' to the base of Glen Burney Falls. While enroute, notice the beautiful boulders on the trail's right side.

This sliding waterfall looks very similar to High Falls, in the Southern Nantahala Wilderness. (See *Waterfall Walks and Drives in Georgia, Alabama, and Tennessee* for directions.) Green algae and mosses adorn the rock at its base. The total height of this waterfall is approximately 30', the lower 8' of which falls vertically, splashing into a small pool. Return to the main trail and continue downstream.

At 1.1 miles reach the top of the second switchback. The trail now makes multiple switchbacks into the gorge. At their base, continue downstream and at 1.2 miles turn right and cross a point of land while enroute to the base of Glen Marie Falls, which lie 80' away.

This 40' (total height) waterfall enters the scene over the left side of a rock exposure, then cascades from right to left. Its waters land amongst large boulders. Mountain magnolia, hemlock and rhododendron cloak the hillsides.

Mile 272 - 268 Blue Ridge Parkway

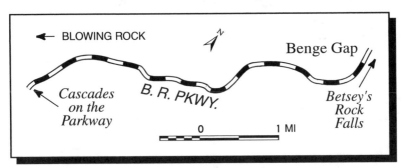

Cascades on the Parkway Loop Trail, Mile 272, Blue Ridge Parkway, Wilkes County, NC

Roads: Paved   A "10" 80'
USGS Quadrangle: Maple Springs, NC, picnic facilities
1 mile round trip, easy-moderate, seasonal restrooms

I almost passed this waterfall up—the name "Cascades" gave me visions of a series of rapids. As is usually the case, my preconceived notions were totally wrong. The "Cascades" are *the* prize gem of the region. I commend the National Park Service for their hard work. Not only was the waterfall a magnificent natural sight, the graveled trail was well maintained, spotless, and informative, as well. Trailside plaques identify many of the trees and flowers found here. Plan a visit of at least two hours, there is so much to see and learn.

Directions: From the town of Blowing Rock, drive north on the Blue Ridge Parkway to milepost 272. The parking area and trailhead are located here. The graveled trail begins at the information board near the restrooms.

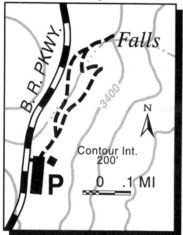

Enter the woods. In 240' arrive at the beginning/end of the loop. (Take the right fork, as directions are described for hiking in a counterclockwise fashion.) After hiking .3 of a mile, reach steps leading down to Falls Creek. Just ahead, the trail crosses a footbridge and soon thereafter joins up with the return portion of the loop, on the left, and the fall's access trail, on the right.

Hike the fall's access trail, which now descends via ramp-like grades and steps. In 200' take the side trail to the observation area atop the falls.

Return to the fall's access trail and hike another 200' to the lower viewpoint.

This is a spectacular waterfall, falling in several slides and tiers with shoals below. From their top, one may see beautiful farms and fields to the east.

To complete the loop, take the previously mentioned return trail, which soon crosses Falls Creek. In .3 of a mile rejoin the inbound portion of the loop. A right turn leads back to the parking area.

Betsey's Rock Falls,
Mile 267.9, Blue Ridge Parkway, Wilkes County, NC

Roads: Paved   A "2"
USGS Quadrangle: Glendale Springs, NC

Located near Benge Gap and Mile 268, this high and slim, ribbonlike waterfall is visible from a parkway overlook. Look for the sign marking their location. To view them, look northeast 1000', or so, across the ravine. The falls may be obscured during the growing season.

Roadside picnic facilities are also located here.

Western South Carolina

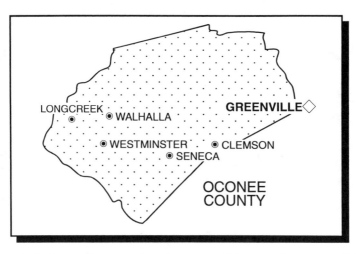

This relatively undiscovered region was a big surprise to me. I had no concept of all the scenery it held in store. This is a land of rolling hills with an occasional "knob" rising high above the surrounding terrain. This is where the foothills end and the Appalachian Mountains begin. Sunday drives abound in this land of day lilies, fine homes, and apple orchards.

South Carolina may not have the lofty mountains of its neighboring state to the north, but it does have some equally stunning waterfalls. The falls covered in this section of the book (unless otherwise noted) are located in Oconee County—South Carolina's "Land of Waterfalls." My favorites are the Falls on Yellow Branch and Lee Falls. Many people consider Lee Falls to be the prettiest in Oconee County. I'm partial to the Falls on Yellow Branch, myself. I urge you to see them both and be your own judge. To see them at their best, go during the week—a time when you'll find few, if any other visitors.

For the "history buff" there is plenty here, too: Historic Oconee Station, the Stumphouse Tunnel, and on the way to Lee Falls, the site on which Revolutionary War hero, General Andrew Pickens, built his home, "Redhouse."

Holly Springs - Longcreek Area

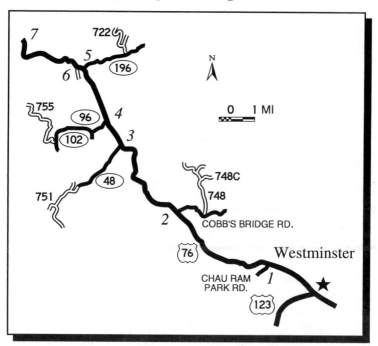

Directions: From the intersection of US Hwys. 76 *West* and 123 *South*, in Westminster, drive west on 76 to the following points of interest:

1. Chau Ram Park Road, access to Ramsey Falls: 2.45 miles.
2. Cobb's Bridge Road, access to Rileymoore Falls: 7.35 miles.
3. Brasstown Road (SR 48), access to Brasstown Falls: 11.9 miles.
4. Damascus Church Road (SR 37-96), access to Long Creek Falls: 13.2 miles.
5. Chattooga Ridge Road (SR 37-196), access to Fall Creek Falls: 15.7 miles.
6. Parking for the Falls on Reedy Branch: 16 miles.
7. The Chattooga River Bridge (GA/SC state line): 17.9 miles.

1. Ramsey Falls, Chau Ram County Park

Roads: Paved   A "4" 37'
Open March through November, camping and full facilities.
USGS Quadrangle: Holly Springs, SC, GA
300' to fall's base area, easy

Directions: From US 76, turn left onto Chau Ram Park Road. In .5 of a mile pass the park office. Just past the office, turn right and head towards the group picnic shelters and trail parking (.65 of a mile from US 76).

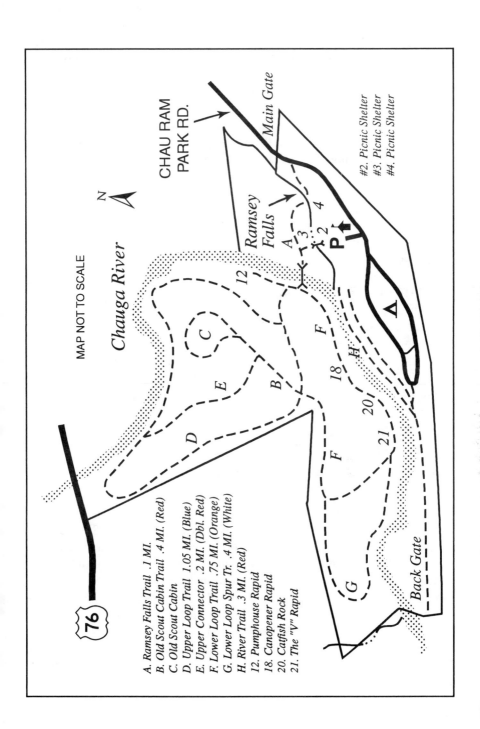

MAP NOT TO SCALE

Chauga River

N

CHAU RAM PARK RD.

Main Gate

Ramsey Falls

#2. Picnic Shelter
#3. Picnic Shelter
#4. Picnic Shelter

A
3
2
4
P

Back Gate

A. Ramsey Falls Trail .1 MI.
B. Old Scout Cabin Trail .4 MI. (Red)
C. Old Scout Cabin
D. Upper Loop Trail 1.05 MI. (Blue)
E. Upper Connector .2 MI. (Dbl. Red)
F. Lower Loop Trail .75 MI. (Orange)
G. Lower Loop Spur Tr. .4 MI. (White)
H. River Trail .3 MI. (Red)
12. Pumphouse Rapid
18. Canopener Rapid
20. Catfish Rock
21. The "V" Rapid

The falls have been the site of several mills over the last 200 years. The first mill was erected by Colonel Alexander Ramsay, in the 1770's. The creek and falls bear his name, which has evolved into *Ramsey* (with an "*E*") over the years.

This park has many features packed into its 75+ acres. Among its rolling hills are more than 3.5 miles of scenic hiking trails. Most of them are rated easy, making them suitable for family hiking. Bouldering (a form of rock climbing) is permitted near the falls. Also popular (near the suspension bridge) is a 100 yard kayaking course, featuring 18 gates. Fishing (state fishing license required) is another of the park's many pluses.

Chau Ram, or nearby Oconee State Park, would make the perfect base camp from which to visit the region's many points of interest.

From the parking area, near the #2 group picnic shelter, cross Ramsey Creek on a footbridge. In 50', at the #3 picnic shelter, the trail splits both left and right. To the right, the Waterfall Trail leads upstream through a maze of boulders, for approximately 250', to a boulder outcrop and viewing area beside Ramsey Falls. After viewing the falls return to the #3 picnic shelter.

From the #3 shelter, the bridge trail leads westerly and in 180' crosses the finest suspension footbridge I've ever set foot on. On its far side (360') the following trails originate:

12. The Pumphouse Rapid Trail: .1 of a mile to the Pumphouse Rapid.
F. The Lower Loop Trail: .3 of a mile to the "V" Rapid.

Other woodland trails spur from these main access routes (see map).

2. Rileymoore Falls

Roads: Graveled/4-WD*   A "6" 8'
USGS Quadrangle: Holly Springs, SC, GA
1.15 miles,   moderate-difficult

Directions: From US 76, drive east on Cobb's Bridge Road for 1.4 miles. Turn left onto Spy Rock Road (FS 748) and drive 1.85 miles to FS 748C. Turn right and continue for just under .1 of a mile to the parking area, which is on the right. The hike begins here, as this road descends very steeply and is badly rutted, in places. *In dry weather the road can be driven in a high-clearance, 4-WD vehicle, to another parking area, .45 of a mile down the mountainside— if you have no phobia about straddling deep ruts.

From the parking area, hike east on 748C. The road bends south as it descends into the Chauga River Valley. In approximately .45 of a mile the road forks. There may be a carsonite stake here stating, "The trail to Rileymoore Falls begins about 300' to the right, by the small parking area." Continue for 300' to the high-clearance, 4-WD parking area*. One hundred feet past the parking area look for the trail's official beginning, which is on the left.

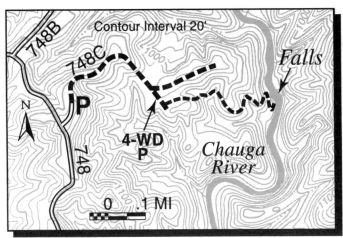

Beginning at an easy to moderate rate, the trail parallels a small branch, which is 25 to 30′ to its right. At .7 of a mile the trail outlines a hollow in a more mature forest. The route soon levels in an area where the forest has recently been harvested. At .8 of a mile the trail bends left to trace the mountainside and soon thereafter turns sharply left, entering then outlining a hollow. The river may be heard, on the right, in this vicinity. In .1 of a mile the trail begins descending steeply and is soon intersected by the old route to the falls. (A steep wash on the left.) At just over a mile arrive at a split. A path leads left and towards the top of the falls, while the *trail* bends right to lead safely to the base. After passing through a designated camping area, turn sharply left at river level (1.1 miles) and hike upstream. The trail terminates at the river's edge (beach area below the falls, 1.15 miles).

Seen from a large beach, adjacent to its blue-green pool, Rileymoore has a very beautiful, rugged appearance. Eight feet high and approximately 80′ wide, the Chauga River first appears in shoaling fashion with boulders breaking its flow. Hardwoods and assorted pines line and overhang the river. The river narrows after pooling and flows out the right side of the plunge pool. The setting is most scenic in the growing season.

This waterfall needs our help. Uncaring campers have chopped trees for firewood and badly littered the beach. Please take a litter bag on this hike.

3. Brasstown Falls

Roads: Graveled   An "8" collectively
USGS Quadrangle: Tugaloo Lake, GA, SC
.2 of a mile, easy-moderate

Note these hazards: poison ivy; a root laced and steep path that is narrow and dangerous below the upper falls.

Directions: From US 76, turn left (south) onto Brasstown Road (SR 37-48). (The pavement ends in 2.7 miles.) After driving a total of 4.1 miles arrive at FS 751. Turn right and drive .5 of a mile to the parking area. The path begins at the jeep-blocking boulders.

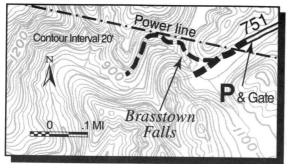

Hike the blocked road and immediately pass under a power line. In 200' the road enters a medium-growth forest. In another 250' veer right at a primitive camping area. (As the roadbed narrows to a single-lane path, the rush of Brasstown Creek can be heard.) Hike an additional 200' to a shoaling Brasstown Creek. The first of three falls lie immediately downstream.

There is a *right* and *wrong* way to the base of each of these falls. The *wrong* way is to attempt *any* route from the top area of either of the three falls. These paths are steep, slick, and dangerous.

The *correct* route is a slim, galax-lined path *farthest* from the creek. This pathway provides access to the base of both the upper and middle falls, then eventually leads steeply to the base of the lower falls.

The upper falls run for 25' and are the more scenic of the three. Lined with mountain rosebay, Brasstown Creek spills from ledge to ledge over a broad rock face then shoals 125', racing to make its next plunge.

Continue downstream and descend a boulder outcrop. Cross a small branch, which joins Brasstown Creek just above the middle tier. Peering through an opening in the rhododendron, enjoy the side view of the middle tier present in this vicinity.

The middle falls resemble a wide and uniform curtain of water with a powerful, sheer drop of 15'. The morning sun's rays show through its mist-laden air. (Approaching the base via a side path, located between the middle and lower tiers, can be a drenching experience.)

The main path now makes a sharp right to circumvent a slide beside the middle falls and its dangerous, exposed drop-offs. Heading inland, towards the power line, the slim path takes a safer route downstream to the lower falls. (The path may be hard to detect in this area, but makes its right turn just before a small, boulder outcrop, adjacent to the middle falls.)

The lower falls tumble for 15' into a bowl-shaped alcove. Its 70', multicolored rock wall plays host to dozens of aquatic plants.

4. Long Creek Falls

Roads: Graveled/High Clearance*   A "6" 20'
USGS Quadrangle: Rainy Mountain, GA, SC
1.65 miles, moderate, (last 600' difficult)

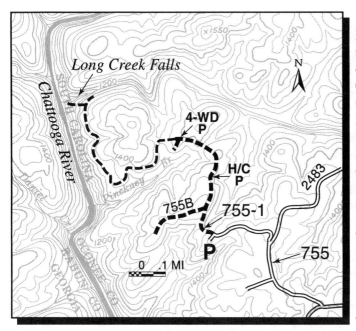

Long Creek Falls

Chattooga River

4-WD
P

H/C
P

755B

755-1

P

755

2483

0   .1 MI

N

Directions: From US 76, turn left (south) onto Damascus Church Road (SR 37-96, the Longcreek Volunteer Fire Dept. is located at this intersection) and drive for .85 of a mile. Turn right onto Battle Creek Road (SR 37-102) and drive 1.9 miles to Turkey Ridge Road (FS 755). Turn right. Continue another 2.95 miles to the graveled parking area on the left. (If you have a high-clearance vehicle and conditions are dry, FS 755-1, on the right, may be driven to a pullout* .4 of a mile ahead.) Since most of us are in automobiles, distances are given from the graveled parking area.

Hike (or drive) 755-1 and in .15 of a mile pass 755B, on the left. In another .25 of a mile pass the high-clearance pullout* (mentioned above) on the right. The road now heads northeast. In 750′ the roadbed encounters a small knob and bends sharply left to head more westerly. Six tenths of a mile into the hike arrive at a turnaround (4-WD parking). The road narrows and continues southwest to another turnaround, used for camping (150′ ahead), while the path to the falls (on the right) leads almost due west (N 80° W) as it enters the woods.

Take the path, which leads down a small wash, and in 150′ pass a diversion channel which drains to the left. Pass over jeep mounds, and with a left bend round the north side of a small knob. The path now adopts a woodland logging road for its treadway. After passing over the narrows of a saddle, at .8 of a mile, the old roadbed swaps sides of the ridge line, to the south face of an unnamed mountain, and parallels the hollow of Pinckney Branch. From this point on, the roadbed outlines each and every hollow enroute to the falls. At just over a mile, enter the Chattooga Wild and Scenic River corridor (denoted by blue painted trees). The muffled sounds of the unseen river are now heard. At 1.05 miles the roadbed makes an abrupt right, to follow the Chattooga upstream.

(Disregard the slim path, on the left, here.) The roadbed now ascends at an easy to moderate rate. It soon levels and outlines a noticeably deeper hollow. At 1.45 miles the treadway begins to descend at an easy to moderate rate. Leveling at 1.5 miles, the roadbed, and the path treading it, peter out amongst the laurel. *(As a landmark, the main path appears to continue straight ahead but becomes impassably overgrown in 150'.)* The rushing waters of Long Creek are heard here. Look carefully for a slim path on the left. This pathway leads steeply downhill, in meandering fashion, and in 600' arrives at the confluence of Long Creek and the Chattooga River, where the falls are viewed.

This is a beautiful, split-flow waterfall with cascades downstream. Located 250 to 300' inland, this is where river runners break for lunch. Alder trees dot its sandy beach area and large boulders are scattered about the creekbed.

This is one of my favorite spots. Not only is there a scenic waterfall, but an awesome river and mountainsides, to boot. The Chattooga enters the scene in a rocky, mountainous run of about 1000'. Placid where Long Creek joins, the river once again churns white in a boulder-filled, downstream course, flowing towards Deliverance Rock. I witnessed a large log balanced atop one of these boulders. Deposited during high water, this log was perched 6 to 8' higher than the normal river level.

Within 300' of this waterfall, I had several photo opportunities: colorful autumn foliage reflecting in and tinting the Chattooga's waters, and beautiful ferns intermingled with colorful leaves kept me busy for hours.

5. Fall Creek Falls

Roads: Graveled   A "5"
USGS Quadrangle: Whetstone, SC, GA
5 minutes, steep-moderate, (no hiking map needed)

Directions: From US 76, take Chattooga Ridge Road (SR 37-196) east for 2.1 miles to Fall Creek Road. Turn left. In .35 of a mile turn left onto FS 722. Drive .5 of a mile to the culvert through which Fall Creek flows. Park in a pullout just ahead on the left.

Walk the road north for 130' (270' from the centerline of the culvert) and look for a noticeable gully (not currently washing) with several logs across it. The fall's pathway enters the woods here and follows the left side of the gully. The pathway then bends slightly right and generally follows or treads this gully to the base. When you arrive creekside, the falls are seen 30' upstream.

The falls are approximately 25' high with a rock face 25' wide. On average, the flow occupies 10 to 15' of its width. Its waters flow into a shallow, sandy pool area.

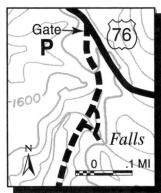

6. Falls on Reedy Branch

Roads: Paved   A "4"   30'
USGS Quadrangle: Rainy Mountain, GA, SC
5 minutes, easy-moderate

Note: An imposing gate at the entry point may give you second thoughts about safe passage. Rest assured, this is public land, having recently been acquired by the Forest Service.

At this location, look for the parking area on the left side of US 76.

Take a path which leads around the left buttress of the gate. The route to the falls treads the graveled road beyond the gate. At 740' arrive at a stone and timber bridge spanning Reedy Branch. Take an old roadbed preceding the bridge that leads upstream to the base area. (The falls soon come into view). At 850' cross to the right side of the creek in the vicinity of the headwall remains of a footbridge. Hike the remaining 100' to the base of the falls. A dilapidated gazebo is testament to its use as a retreat by its former owners.

With adequate rainfall this is a very pretty waterfall. Thirty-feet high, it cascades in dozens of tiers over moss-covered bedrock. The rock face and cliffs, on the right, show evidence of having once been a quarry (bore holes).

7. The Chattooga River Bridge (GA/SC line) as above.

Walhalla West

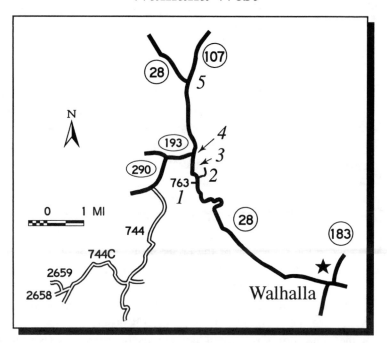

Directions: From the intersection of SC Hwys. 28 (Main St.) and 183 *North*, in Walhalla, drive north on SC 28 to the following points of interest:
1. The Yellow Branch Picnic Area (FS 763), access to the Falls on Yellow Branch: 5.5 miles.
2. Stumphouse Tunnel Road (SR 37-226), access to Issaqueena Falls: 5.6 miles.
3. The US Forest Service Stumphouse Ranger Station: 6 miles.
4. Whetstone Road (SR 193), access to Cedar Creek Falls - Blue Hole Falls: 6.3 miles.
5. The intersection of SC Hwys. 28 and 107: 8.3 miles. (Also see Nicholson and Burrell's Ford Areas pg. 140.)

1. Falls on Yellow Branch

Roads: Paved   A "10+" 60'
USGS Quadrangle: Whetstone, SC, GA
No formal trail, 1 mile to base, shallow water crossings, poison ivy, moderate

Note: This grand spectacle takes extra ability in the pathfinding department. The hike initially treads a loop trail, then takes a woodland path the remaining distance to the falls. The path is easy to discern, in places, then in

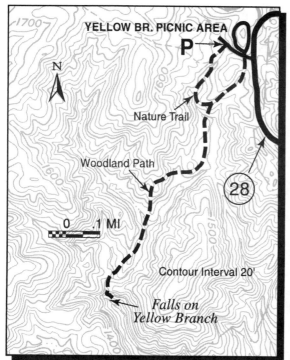

others seems to vanish. Hang tough, it's worth every effort!

Directions: From SC 28, turn left into the Yellow Branch Picnic Area. Drive less than .1 of a mile to the pullout on the left. Park here. (If you cross Yellow Branch and enter the parking lot for the #2 picnic area, you've gone too far.) The trail may be marked by a sign, 100' or so, due south, reading, "nature trail." If the sign is missing, look for a small, collapsed rock bridge and cross Yellow Branch over *it* to begin your hike.

Hike downstream paralleling Yellow Branch and crossing the creek *four* times. One-fourth mile into the hike, where the loop trail veers left (east), away from Yellow Branch, look carefully for a faint path on the right (south side). This pathway leads to the falls. (A 16-18" maple tree with a knee- to waist-high, 8" by 2' blaze stood at this location at the time of my last visit. If this cannot be found, look for a couple of faint paths that descend the point of land between Yellow Branch and the unnamed branch [on the left]. These paths converge into a more discernible route on the bank of Yellow Branch.) (The loop trail continues for .2 of a mile and ties into the inbound road near the #1 picnic area.)

Hike the side path and in 135' cross Yellow Branch. The path now treads the creek's right (west) side, in the level creek bottom, through woods that are somewhat open. After passing within eyesight of the creek, while rounding the foot of a ridge, tread an old roadbed (.45 of a mile) while passing under a canopy of laurel. Just ahead, where the roadbed becomes overgrown, with a left turn, the path leaves the roadbed and descends in "S" fashion. The path now enters another open wooded area with stands of oak, maple and poplar, and at .5 of a mile crosses a small tributary branch. Winding and undulating, encounter a bumper crop of ferns and a rhododendron thicket. At .7 of a mile cross another small branch then pass through heavy windfalls. At .8 of a mile the pathway leaves Yellow Branch and climbs a small ridge. After topping out, the route descends its west slope then crosses a small branch at its confluence with Yellow Branch. A small pool is located here. Approximately 200' downstream from the pool, cross Yellow Branch on shallow bedrock. (The path is hard to discern here, as hikers have taken different routes across the creek.) Now on the east side of the creek, continue downstream for 200' to the top of the falls. As you near them, the correct route leads up the hill slightly, and away from the top area. The top has several hazards: first, it's 60' straight down; and second, a bumper crop of industrial-strength poison ivy. Hazards aside, there is a fine view of the forest below.

To reach the base, take the steep and muddy path, on the left, downstream another 250'.

The rocks at the base are moss covered. The falls are in a most beautiful woodland setting with lots of rhododendron, large poplars, oaks, and hemlock. Where the rock face is exposed by the creek's flow, multi colors of brown show through.

2. Issaqueena Falls

Roads: Paved   A "10" 50'
USGS Quadrangle: Walhalla, SC
.1 of a mile, 10 minutes, moderate
Open 8:00 a.m. to dusk, poison ivy, (no hiking map needed)

This beauty is located within South Carolina's historic, Stumphouse Tunnel Park. Stumphouse Mountain is the site of a failed 1850's railroad tunneling venture. The Blue Ridge Railroad Company had plans to connect Charleston, SC, with Cincinnati, Ohio. A series of three tunnels were begun in this area. Only "Middle Tunnel," the shortest (385') was completed. The project was put on hold in 1859 when funds dried up. The Civil War dealt it a death blow, and work was never resumed.

Of the three tunnels, only Stumphouse Tunnel (now sealed due to rockfall) is accessible. Stumphouse Tunnel was to be 5863' long. Only 1600' of it was completed. The work was performed by Irishmen, progressing 200' a month, using hand tools and black powder.

There is a story behind Issaqueena Falls, as well. Legend has it, that an Indian maiden, who married a white trader, jumped from the falls to her death, to escape persecution from her tribe. Another version of the story says that she jumped from the top of the falls, to a ledge below, then under the cover of darkness fled to Alabama to join her husband. No matter what the story, the falls are a legendary beauty when seen from the base.

Directions: Turn right onto a winding and steeply-descending Stumphouse Tunnel Road (SR 37-226). Drive .4 of a mile and turn right into the fall's picnic area. Park at the apex of this loop road.

Hike south for 200' to the top of the falls. There's not much to see from this vantage point—just another creek flowing over a cliff. The mood is altered altogether enroute to the base. The setting changes to one of being deep in the woods.

To reach the base, take the pathway crossing the footbridge on the *west* side of the parking lot. In approximately 400' arrive at a side path on the left. Take this path for 200' to the base of the falls.

Hundreds of small trickles race down the granite face of this natural masterpiece.

Stumphouse Tunnel

To visit the tunnel, return to Stumphouse Tunnel Road and drive north .2 of a mile to the gate. Park, then hike 300' to its opening. During wet weather, notice a small cascade to the left of the opening (Tunnel Falls).

3. The Stumphouse Ranger Station (as above).

4. Cedar Creek Falls - Blue Hole Falls

Roads: Graveled*   A "4" & A "4"
USGS Quadrangle: Whetstone, SC, GA
.55 of a mile, water crossing, moderate

Note: I visited these waterfalls during a summer dry spell. The creek crossing at the shoals (between the falls, see below) was ankle deep. A little rain makes this crossing a treacherous one. I urge extreme caution here at all times, but especially during high water conditions.

Directions: From SC 28, take Whetstone Road (SR 193) west for .7 of a mile to Cassidy Bridge Road (SR 290). Turn left and drive .9 of a mile to Rich Mountain Road (FS 744). Turn left again and drive 3.35 miles to FS 744C. Turn right and continue for 2.55 miles to the single-lane and very badly rutted FS 2658, which is on the right. Park on the left side of 744C at this intersection. (If you end up at the cul-de-sac on 744C, you've passed 2658 by .15 of a mile.) *Travel from here on should be made in a high-clearance, 4-WD vehicle, or on foot. Since most of us are in automobiles, we'll begin the hike here.

Hike the moderately descending and badly rutted FS 2658. In .25 of a mile veer sharply right onto a level but winding FS 2659. With Blue Hole resonating through the woods, continue another .25 of a mile to a pullout on the left side of the road. Look for a slim path on the left, leading into the woods. Hike this steeply-descending path and in 120' exit the woods on bedrock at creek level. Cedar Creek Falls lie upstream 100', or so.

This waterfall is broader than it is high, and despite heavy visitation still has an unspoiled appearance. The creek slides 8-10' down the rock face, pools,

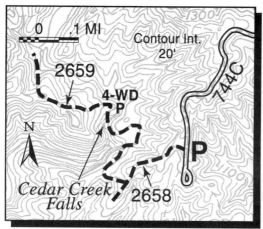

then shoals its way downstream to Blue Hole Falls, which from this vantage point is hidden from view. Notice the potholed rock over which Cedar Creek flows before dropping out of sight.

To reach Blue Hole Falls, return to the spot where you first arrived at creek level. Look for the shallowest route across the creek. (You can see the worn track most people have taken to cross it.) On the west bank, carefully walk the dry portion of the bedrock downstream. In approximately 30' the path reenters the woods and leads steeply downhill to a viewpoint alongside Blue Hole Falls.

Despite being fairly easy to reach, these waterfalls have a rugged beauty about them. The mountainsides are steep and cloaked in laurel and rhododendron.

5. SC Hwys. 28 and 107 (as above).

Nicholson and Burrell's Ford Areas

Note: I have hiked the Chattooga River Trail (CRT) from Burrell's Ford downstream to the Nicholson Ford access. I measured a total distance of 9 miles. The CRT is rugged, especially between Big Bend Falls and the Falls on the Chattooga River above Rock Gorge. I therefore recommend, that you go in from either end, and return to that respective trailhead, instead of trying to connect all the way through.

Directions: From the intersection of SC Hwys. 28 and 107, northwest of Walhalla, drive north on 107 the following distances to these points of interest:

1. Oconee State Park: 2.5 miles.
2. Station Mtn. Road (FS 716), access to Hidden Falls: 3 miles.
3. Village Creek Road, access to (a) Lick Log Creek Falls, and (b) the Falls on the Chattooga River above Rock Gorge: 3.5 miles.
4. Cheohee Road (FS 710, shown on the quadrangle as Tamassee Road), access to shuttle parking for the Winding Stairs Trail: 6.25 miles. Take Cheohee Road for 3.4 miles to shuttle parking at the trail's lower end.

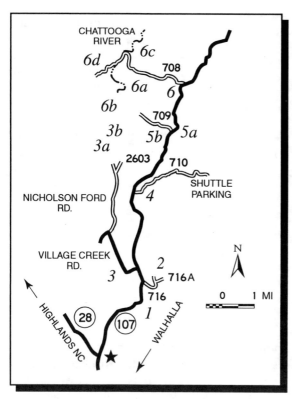

5. Parking for (a) the Winding Stairs Trail (Miuka Falls), and (b) the Big Bend Trail (alternate route to Big Bend Falls): 8.65 miles.

6. Burrell's Ford Road (FS 708), access to (a) King Creek Falls, (b) Big Bend Falls, and (c) Spoonauger Falls; (d) the Chattooga River Bridge: 10.4 miles.

1. Oconee State Park (as above).

2. Hidden Falls

Roads: Graveled   A "2" 60' in two tiers
USGS Quadrangle: Tamassee, SC, GA
1.25 miles, moderate

Note: Best seen after substantial rainfall.

While not the most scenic waterfall in the book, the hike is exceptional in spring and more so in the fall. Laurels bloom early on these east-facing slopes. For the same reason, fall arrives a little late. Hickory, maple, oak, and tupelo fluoresce in the colors of fall, with lesser amounts of pine adding an element of starkness.

Directions: From SC 107, turn right (east) onto Station Mtn. Road (FS 716). Drive 1 mile and turn right onto FS 716A (shown on the quadrangle as FS 715-2). Look for the parking area 200' ahead, on the right. The hike begins at the guardrail which barricades the road.

Initially descending the grassy roadbed, in 75' cross the Foothills Trail.

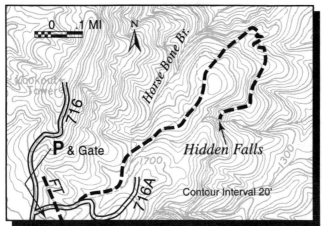

After hiking the Hidden Falls Trail for 470′, veer left, leaving the open roadbed in "Y" fashion, and enter the forest to tread a woodland road. (The open road continues straight ahead then bends sharply right.)

From this point, the trail descends the right side of a hollow via the woodland road. At the quarter-mile point, the trail crosses the hollow and a small branch rising in it. At .3 of a mile cross another small branch rising in a second hollow. In the area around .35 of a mile the trail parallels the newly formed fall's branch (on the right). The trail soon levels, straightens, and distances itself from the branch. In this vicinity, to the left, the hollow of Horse Bone Branch opens up and deepens, while the trail traverses the ridge line separating Horse Bone and Hidden Falls branches. At .65 of a mile the trail makes a right and left jog as the roadbed becomes overgrown and peters out. (Although the roadbed is still shown on the quadrangle, it is now undetectable in the field.) The trail now meanders amongst laurel and small hardwoods as it rounds the west side of a small knob. Rounding the knob's north and east slopes, excellent highland views are presented through the open woods of winter. While rounding the east slope, at .9 of a mile, the trail switchbacks then enters and outlines a couple of small hollows, the slopes of which are covered thickly in laurel and rhododendron. Now heading generally south, at 1.1 miles the trail turns uphill to cross a sloping ridge line. On the gently-winding descent of the south slope, enter a stand of large hardwoods. The fall's glistening rock becomes visible on the left. After hiking a total of 1.25 miles arrive at the base of Hidden Falls.

With adequate water the falls are quite impressive—in the dry months they are little more than dripping, moist rock. Although I have not visited them in the summertime, I feel they would be most picturesque *then*—again, only if there has been adequate rainfall.

Hidden Falls drops a total of 60′ in two major tiers. The falls first appear as a 5′ cascade which then drops 10′, splashing onto bedrock. Spilling from this first landing, the creek is split into a score of rivulets. The creek then widens and free falls 8′, splashing onto bedrock, where it cascades for the rest of its run. Large boulders at its base afford a frontal view.

The falls are best photographed on a cloudy day and after heavy rainfall.

3a. Lick Log Creek Falls

Roads: Graveled   A "6" & "4" respectively
USGS Quadrangles: Satolah, Tamassee, SC, GA, in their margins
Yellow and white blazed, 1.15 miles to lower falls, moderate

Directions: From SC 107, turn left (west) onto Village Creek Road and drive 1.75 miles to Nicholson Ford Road. Turn right and drive 2.1 miles, passing the Bartram/Foothills trail overnight parking area and Pribyl Road, while enroute to the intersection of Thrift Lake Road (private) and FS 2603 (a fork). Veer right onto 2603. The parking area is .15 of a mile ahead. The trail begins at its northeast corner.

Upper Falls

The Bartram/Foothills trail enters the woods and immediately passes the fisherman's register. With a hollow to its right the trail treads level, at first, passing through a forest consisting primarily of conifers. At 300' the trail begins descending at an easy rate while bending left to round the mountainside. Exiting a hollow, at just over a quarter mile, the trail bends left then straightens. The muffled sound of Pigpen Branch is now heard on the right. With a slight left-trending meander, the trail soon parallels this creek. At the half-mile point pass a fire ring (on the right). The trail bends left at this primitive campsite and crosses a footbridge over Lick Log Creek, 60' upstream from its confluence with Pigpen Branch. The trail then enters a stand of large hemlocks with a fire ring among them. At .6 of a mile cross to the north side of Lick Log Creek on a footbridge. The trail now treads a descending roadbed alongside Lick Log Creek. At .7 of a mile pass a side path leading to the base of Lick Log Falls. Continue straight ahead to the official tie-in with the CRT (.75 of a mile)*. At this trail intersection the CRT leads both north and south. Hike the CRT downstream (south) and in 430' arrive at the footbridge crossing of Lick Log Creek. Upper Lick Log Falls are seen from a viewing area 30' upstream from the bridge.

This is a cascading waterfall with a run of 50'. Its upper level is obscured from view but falls approximately 10'. As well, the lower tier falls 10'. The lower tier is split in half by the bedrock, with a more vertical flow on the left and a lengthy, cascading flow on the right. A large pool lies at its base (approximately 50' wide and 35' towards the viewer, from its entry point). Laurel, with interesting shapes, and rhododendron surround the falls and pool. On the right side of the viewing area, a large sandstone boulder juts out of the earth at a 15° angle. American holly clutches its right side.

Middle and Lower Falls

To reach the middle and lower falls, backtrack 30'(return) to the footbridge and cross Lick Log Creek. The CRT meanders downstream alongside Lick Log Creek, albeit at a distance, through the doghobble, in a hemlock forest. Two tenths of a mile from the bridge enter the Chattooga Wild and Scenic River corridor (blue painted trees). The trail once again nears the creek and at .25 of a mile passes alongside the middle falls.

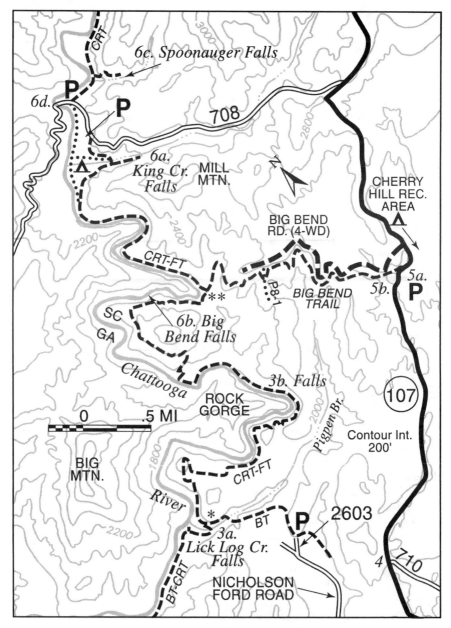

6c. Spoonauger Falls

CRT

6d.

P

P

708

6a. King Cr. Falls

MILL MTN.

N

CHERRY HILL REC. AREA

BIG BEND RD. (4-WD)

CRT-FT

P8-1

BIG BEND TRAIL

5a.

5b.

P

SC GA

6b. Big Bend Falls

**

Chattooga

3b. Falls

ROCK GORGE

(107)

BIG MTN.

0   .5 MI

CRT-FT

Pigpen Br.

Contour Int. 200'

River

*

BT

P

2603

3a. Lick Log Cr. Falls

BT-CRT

NICHOLSON FORD ROAD

4

710

Seen through an opening, the middle falls lie approximately 100' away. Broader (20') than they are high (15'), this foaming, white water cascade (upper tier) is approximately 10° from being vertical. The creek then runs 30' and once again cascades over bedrock in a 6' fall. The total run of both tiers is approximately 70'.

Continuing downstream, at .3 of a mile the CRT turns sharply left. Look for a slim path (on the right) descending a laurel-covered point of land. Hike this steep and winding path for 200' to the base of Lower Lick Log Falls.

View the falls from a gravelly beach at the river's edge. The lower falls are of the sliding variety. Panning from right to left, the slide lengthens to 30' as its waters slip into a small pool and soon thereafter join the Chattooga.

*See Falls on the Chattooga River above Rock Gorge.

3b. Falls on the Chattooga River above Rock Gorge

Roads/Quadrangle: See Lick Log Creek   A "6" 15'
Black blaze, 3.1 miles from the Lick Log parking area,   moderate-difficult

This trail gains approximately 300' in elevation as it goes up and over a ridge then descends into the Chattooga River Gorge. (For most of the hike the river is unseen.) In doing so, the trail bypasses the Chattooga's impassable Square Bends and Rock Gorge.

At the intersection of the Foothills/Bartram and Chattooga River trails*, hike north (following the CRT/FT upstream). Level, at first, the trail soon ascends at a moderate rate. At .3 of a mile outline a sharp, steep-sided hollow. Just shy of .4 of a mile, the trail makes a hard right and heads northeasterly, ascending a ridge line, with a small hollow to the left. Atop a saddle (.55 of a mile) the trail makes a sharp right to head south. Having attained the ridge, that separates the Chattooga River and Pigpen Branch drainages, the trail now skirts the meandering Wild and Scenic River boundary for the next mile. This is denoted by blue painted trees. At 1.55 miles, while heading northerly, cross into the Chattooga Wild and Scenic River corridor. Now descending, at a point of land (1.7 miles) the trail turns more easterly and the still unseen river is heard far below. After outlining three small, but prominent hollows, arrive near river level (2.1 miles). While on this leg you may catch a glimpse of the river to the north. (Where the river bends left, then disappears, is our objective.) Traveling upstream, the trail undulates and the hillsides steepen, allowing only a narrow treadway. After crossing the *second* of two small branches (both in the vicinity of 2.3 miles) the trail is once again in the proximity of river level. Access to a beach-like area lies 135' ahead. Take an obscure side path for 90' to the river's edge where only the lower left portion of the falls are seen.

The main attraction here is the beautiful river: lots of rock and white water, clear and deep pools tinted from green to indigo, and the small, but magnificent cliffs to the Georgia side.

For a full view of the falls, return to the main trail and hike upstream approximately 200'. Once there, carefully scramble down the exploratory path to the river's edge where this violent waterfall is seen from its side.

The falls are constricted by a boulder outcrop and bedrock on the South Carolina side and boulders that have fallen into the river on the Georgia side. Massive logs hang in its flowway. Its waters churn a foaming, green-white at the base.

*See Upper Lick Log Creek Falls for directions to this point.

4. Cheohee Road (as above).

5a. Miuka (Cheohee) Falls, (Winding Stairs Trail)

Roads: Paved/Graveled   A "3"
USGS Quadrangle: Tamassee, SC, GA
Trail #20, red blazed, minor water crossings, 1.25 miles to falls, 3.45 miles
to FS 710 (shuttle parking), easy, when hiked as described.

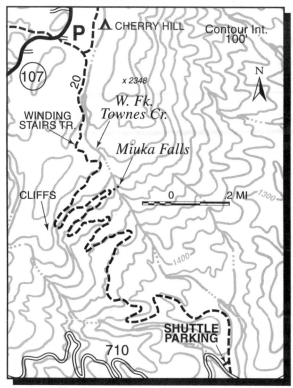

At this location the Winding Stairs Trail begins on the right side of the parking area (an unmarked, barricaded Forest Service road, shown on the quadrangle as FS 735).

The trail enters the woods heading due south. Initially ascending at an easy to moderate rate, at 440' the trail tops the ridge and begins an equal rate of descent. At approximately .15 of a mile the trail levels in a wide hollow. At the quarter mile the trail bends sharply right as a path from the Cherry Hill Recreation Area joins from the left. The trail now treads an old logging road under a canopy of rhododendron with a hollow on the left. In the hollow the West Fork of Townes Creek rises. Sparse hemlocks dot this highland terrain. At one third of a mile cross a jeep-blocking mound. The trail now descends the wide roadbed within earshot of the newborn creek. While exiting a right bend (.65 of a mile) a succession of three silvery lakes are seen through the open woods of winter (S 30° E). This is the top of the first switchback.

At the switchback's midpoint (.95 of a mile) the trail makes a sharp left bend just prior to a 60' rock cliff. The cliff face shows the drill marks of having once been a quarry. During my winter hike this edifice was decorated with 4 to 6' icicles. Likewise, the rock is moss covered.

146

Continuing to descend, pass a large boulder to the trail's left. As it is approached this boulder has an amazing resemblance to a dog's head. For that reason I have dubbed it "Hound Dog Rock." Fall color is hard to beat here.

At 1.2 miles reach the bottom of the *first* and top of the *second* switchback. In the midpoint of this bend, look for a barely discernible path, on the left, that descends steeply for just over 100' to Miuka Falls.

The falls are just barely visible from the main trail which also provides the safest spot from which to view them. In summer, they may be virtually impossible to see because of all the deciduous trees blocking the view. If you venture down to their base, however, you'll find that they're very beautiful but obscured by laurel and rhododendron. *Do not venture onto the creek's bedrock trying to get a better view, as it is treacherously slick.*

The granite over which the creek flows, has ornate quartz swirls. The falls consist of two major tiers. The upper tier is a broken cascade that slopes 30° back into the mountain, falling in 7 to 10'breaks. The lower portion slides then falls with its waters landing on a tilted bedrock exposure (10-12'high on the left, and 8'on the right). Winter views of the previously mentioned lakes are present at the base, as well.

Being less traveled from Miuka Falls, the Winding Stairs Trail narrows significantly, although it still treads the roadbed. The trail terminates at FS 710 in another 2.2 miles. (See shuttle directions pg. 140.)

5b. Big Bend Falls via The Big Bend Trail

Note: See hiking map pg. 144.

This hike is for those who want an alternative to the Chattooga River Trail. It is also a good shuttle exit point for those who want to hike the CRT downstream from Burrell's Ford or upstream from the Lick Log Creek area. As well, when icy conditions are prevalent along the CRT, between Burrell's Ford and the Big Bend Trail, this would be the route to take to Big Bend Falls. The trail's highlights are listed below.

The Big Bend Trail shares the same parking area with the Winding Stairs Trail. The hike begins on the west side of SC 107.

- 0.0: Enter the woods on the west side of SC 107.
- .25 of a mile: Cross to Crane Creek's south side on a footbridge.
- .5 of a mile: Pass through a saddle and outline the high end of a couple of small hollows.
- .7 to 1.7 miles: Outline the hollows from which Pigpen Branch rises.
- 1.75 miles: Make a diagonal crossing of FS road P8-1. As you cross, look for a fisherman's register on the right. (This is a confusing spot. A pathway treads this roadbed from northeast to southwest and leads to the Chattooga in the vicinity of the Falls on the Chattooga River above Rock Gorge.)

• 2.3 miles: Enter the Chattooga Wild and Scenic River corridor and immediately cross the overgrown remains of Big Bend Road.

• 2.5 miles: Cross an unnamed but substantial creek on steppingstones. In just over 50′ the trail turns sharply left to follow it downstream. (This is another confusing spot. It appears that many hikers miss this turn and head, erroneously, for a primitive campsite that lies just out of view straight ahead.) In 30′ the trail confusingly recrosses the creek and heads down its south side.

• 2.7 miles: Intersect the CRT near a footbridge** over the creek we have been following.

(**See hiking map and item 6(b) [Big Bend Falls] for further directions.)

6(a) King Creek and (b) Big Bend Falls

Roads: Graveled   A "7" & A "5" respectively
USGS Quadrangle: Tamassee, SC, GA
See text for distances, easy to difficult

Note: See hiking map pg. 144.

Directions: From SC 107, drive west on Burrell's Ford Road (FS 708) for 2.35 miles to the Burrell's Ford Campground parking area, which is on the left. Locate the information board at the southwest corner of the parking area. The trail begins behind it, and carries the black blaze of the Chattooga River Trail as well as the white blaze of the Foothills Trail.

Hike this curvaceous trail and in .45 of a mile the red-blazed trail from the Burrell's Ford Campground joins from the right. The route now descends and in 60′ crosses King Creek on a footbridge. On the creek's south side, the red-blazed King Creek Falls Trail soon departs to the left (upstream, .55 of a mile) while the black- and white-blazed Chattooga River/Foothills Trail continues to the right (downstream). Hike an undulating and ascending .25 of a mile to the fall's rocky viewing area.

King Creek is a super beautiful waterfall, made more so by winter and spring rains. Housed in a U-shaped cove, its rock walls are almost vertical. In the warm months the falls sport the greenest of mosses.

To reach Big Bend Falls return to the CRT/FT.

From the King Creek Falls Trail junction, the CRT/FT treads high above King Creek. Drifting inland, in 690′ enter the Chattooga Wild and Scenic River corridor, denoted by blue painted trees. Soon thereafter, outline a hollow. Exiting the hollow the trail bends sharply left, straightens somewhat, and descends to intersect the old Chattooga River Trail (.95 of a mile from the parking area) which leads up river to the campground.

Heading down river, with the Chattooga veiled from view, the trail winds and undulates, descending close to river level. At 1.2 miles arrive at the fisherman's register. In the straightaway below the register there are several shoals and rock outcrops painted with lichens. The river's sandy banks sport cinnamon ferns and galax aplenty. At 1.6 miles cross a small creek on a one-lane wooden footbridge. In a deep river bend (1.7 miles) arrive at a high point with equidistant views both up and downstream. With a meandering ascent the trail drifts away from the river. After passing a couple of noticeable rock outcrops, arrive at the top of the first descending switchbacks (2 miles). At river level (2.05 miles) head downstream. At 2.2 miles arrive at the sunning rocks. This bedrock landmark projects 3 to 4' out of the water and extends almost the complete width of the river. In the straightaway preceding the Big Bend the trail is very close to river level. At 2.55 miles cross a small creek and pass an elevated, primitive campsite to the trail's left. At 2.6 miles arrive at a near impassable bedrock outcrop. The steep mountainsides force the trail to traverse two-hundred feet of bedrock beside the fast-running river. This often presents a formidable obstacle, especially after rain or when icy. (See "Trail Mishappenings," in the book's introduction.) Reentering the woods the trail is rocky and sports slick roots, but soon becomes more conducive to hiking. At 2.9 miles arrive at the footbridge and creek preceding the Big Bend Trail. In 35' arrive at the Big Bend Trail intersection** (signs point out the various routes). Ascending, at 2.95 miles, cross the disused Big Bend Road. At 3.05 miles enjoy through-the-trees views of the river far below (perhaps 200 to 300' in elevation). At 3.15 miles, with a right turn, the trail makes a lengthy, descending switchback. After meandering and regaining the high ground, with a right turn (3.6 miles) descend in switchback fashion. Sixty-five feet beyond the base of this switchback look for a side path that leads 100', or so, to the side view of Big Bend Falls.

Note the massive, rock overhang to the right side of the falls.

(**For directions see hiking map and item (5b.), [the Big Bend Trail].)

6c. Spoonauger Falls

Roads: Graveled   An "8"
USGS Quadrangle: Tamassee, SC, GA
.35 of a mile, 15 minutes, easy-moderate

Note: See hiking map pg. 144.
Best seen after rainfall.

In the past, I have underrated the beauty of this waterfall. My previous visits were made during the dry months. While other nearby waterfalls had adequate water, Spoonauger didn't. In fact, it was little more than a trickle over wet rock. During a recent midwinter visit my opinion changed 180°. The winter was an especially wet one and there had been better than 1" of rainfall two days before. This transformed the normally mediocre waterfall into one of the most beautiful I've seen.

Directions: See the directions to King Creek and Big Bend falls parking, and travel west on 708 for an additional .3 of a mile to the parking area for the Chattooga River Trail, which is on the right.

Hike the Chattooga River Trail *upstream* and in .2 of a mile cross Spoonauger Creek on steppingstones. In 70', with a right turn, take the fall's side trail. This trail parallels the creek upstream for a short distance, then turns left to switchback up the mountainside. From several high vantage points beautiful falls are seen below. After hiking .35 of a mile arrive at the viewing area for Spoonauger Falls.

Spoonauger Creek spills out of the rhododendron in a progressively steepening cascade of 40'. In full flow its coverage is approximately 20' of the 40'-wide rock face. Housed in a steep cove, this waterfall has beautiful rock to its left. Hemlocks top it and flank its sides. Downstream, the creek is totally obscured by thick rhododendron.

6d. The Chattooga River Bridge

For the anglers among you, the Chattooga's Burrell's Ford access lies .15 of a mile from CRT parking for Spoonauger Falls (2.8 miles from SC 107).

Walhalla North

Directions: From the intersection of SC 28 and SC 183 *North*, in Walhalla,

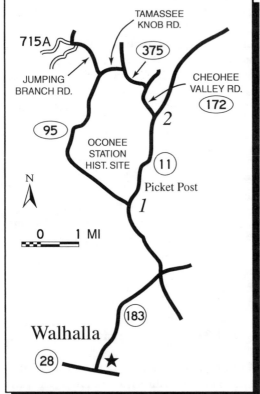

drive north on 183 for 3.55 miles to SC 11. Take Hwy. 11 north to the following points of interest:

1. Oconee Station Road (SR 95, sign: "Oconee Station State Historic Site"), access to Station Cove Falls: 2.1 miles.

2. Cheohee Valley Road (SR 172), access to Lee Falls: 4.5 miles. See the text for further directions.

1. Station Cove Falls

Roads: Paved   A "7" 60'
USGS Quadrangle: Walhalla, SC
.7 of a mile, minor water crossing, easy

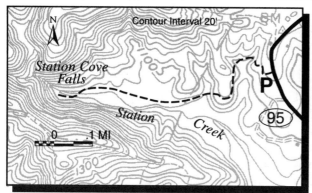

Directions: Turn left onto Oconee Station Road (SR 95) and check your mileage. In 2.1 miles, pass historic Oconee Station* which is on the right. Continue for another .2 of a mile (2.3 miles total) to a small, off-the-road parking area on the left. The fall's trail begins here.

From the jeep-blocking barricades, this well maintained trail (an old logging road) enters the woods and descends while bending in an "S" fashion. At .1 of a mile the trail bends sharply left and drops to cross a small branch on a footbridge. Approximately .2 of a mile into the hike pass alongside a swamp created by industrious beavers. At .4 of a mile cross a footbridge over a small, year-round creek. Station Creek is soon seen flowing lazily through the woods. In summer, this sylvan setting is deeply shaded and cool, with bloodroot and Mayapple covering the forest floor. In another .2 of a mile arrive at Station Creek. Cross the creek on steppingstones. (Do not take the path on the right side of the creek, as it soon dead-ends and leaves you having to cross the creek upstream on slick rock.) Hike an additional .1 of a mile to the viewing area and base of the falls.

The first plunge is approximately 10-12' followed by a 30 footer that splits Station Creek's waters into a half-dozen flows. Adorned with exquisite mosses, beautiful brown rock shows through the flow area of this low-country waterfall. The creek then slides, pools, and shoals downstream, channeled over and through bedrock, to the crossing encountered on the way in. There are large boulders on its left side and lots of hardwoods (oak and poplar) up its cove. Beautiful cliffs flank the fall's right side.

Oconee Station State Historic Site

While in the area, visit historic Oconee Station. (*See directions above.)

Oconee Station was one of seven outposts authorized by the South Carolina General Assembly, in the 1750's, to protect western frontier settlements from Indian attacks. The outpost was home to thirty militia-men at a time, and soon became a thriving center of trade. Two of the original buildings, one of which was owned by a prosperous trader (and are the oldest in Oconee County, dating to around 1800), are still intact.

Park hours are 9 a.m. to 6 p.m. Closed Monday—Wednesday.

2. Lee Falls

Roads: Graveled   A "10" 40'
USGS Quadrangle: Tamassee, SC
1.6 miles, 1 hour, water crossings, difficult

Note: I hiked to this waterfall in the summertime. Had the wildlife openings not recently been mowed, I would've been walking through almost hip-deep grasses and vines. I would therefore recommend that you hike to Lee Falls on a mild winter's day or before new growth occurs in the spring.

Directions: Turn left (west) onto Cheohee Valley Road (SR 172, this changes to SR 375 in just over a mile) and drive 2.2 miles to Tamassee Knob Road (SR 95). Turn left and continue for .5 of a mile to Jumping Branch Road (County Hwy. 9). Turn right and drive 1.45 miles to FS 715A, on the left. Travel 715A (a one-lane graveled road) for .7 of a mile to the concrete ford and culvert-like bridge over Tamassee Creek. Prior to crossing the creek, turn right (upstream) onto an unimproved road and drive 200' to the parking area. The gate (guardrail), where the hike begins, is approximately 50' further upstream.

For the most part, the path to the falls treads an old roadbed that follows Tamassee Creek upstream.

The path immediately enters and passes to the creek side of a tilled field (wildlife opening) that is often planted in corn or soybeans. In .2 of a mile the road (path) veers left, enters the woods briefly, and crosses Tamassee Creek to the south bank. At the quarter-mile enter and pass through another wildlife opening with a test planting of hardwoods. At .4 of a mile arrive at a third wildlife opening. (Hike the tree line on the high side of this field for easier going.) At .55 of a mile enter the woods on the west side of the field and immediately cross Tamassee Creek. (The paths converge into a more discernible, tunnellike opening in the tree line, and cross to the north side of the creek [a wet, steppingstone crossing]). The pathway then enters another cultivated wildlife opening (the fourth). Walk the high side of this field, as well. Seven-tenths of a mile into the hike, the path leaves the field, entering the woods (easily missed) on its northwest side.

At .95 of a mile the path turns more noticeably uphill and narrows to a single track. In 300' look carefully to the left for the narrow path to the falls which now leaves the roadbed. (At the time of my last visit, hikers had blocked off the roadbed here.) In approximately 200' the path dips to cross a small, unnamed branch, while passing through rhododendron. This soon gives way to a stretch heavy with poison ivy. (The path is hard to discern in this vicinity, on account of the heavy vegetation.) The mountainsides soon close in on the right. At 1.25 miles cross a small, unnamed branch, and arrive at the pointed base of a ridge. (There is a fire ring at the base of this point of land,

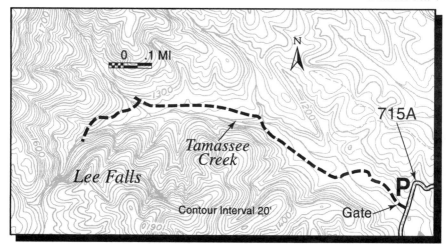

and a path leading steeply up the mountainside—disregard the path.) In 80′ cross to the left side of Tamassee Creek. One and three-tenths miles into the hike, pass the ruins of a gold smelter, on the left (mound of dirt). The path peters out here. For the next .2 of a mile it's hunt and peck hiking, through the rhododendron, up the creek, and over boulders and fallen logs.

The falls are in a very steep, rocky cove with the aforementioned rhododendron, hardwoods, mountain magnolia and some hemlock in residence, as well. Mosses of every hue of green adorn the cliff face.

The best photographic conditions exist on an overcast day with its diffused lighting.

Local History

During the Revolutionary War, the Cherokee raided white settlements in the area while local Patriots were in the coastal Carolinas fighting the British. General Andrew Pickens, and his forces, came to the area to quash the raids. General Pickens so liked the area, that he made it his home. His residence, "Redhouse" sat atop a hill located at the intersection of Tamassee Knob and Jumping Branch roads. A boulder and plaque, placed by The Daughters of the American Revolution, marks the spot.

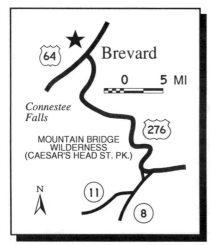

Brevard South

Connestee Falls, Transylvania County, NC

Roads: Paved   A "6"
USGS Quadrangle: Brevard, NC, SC
Seen from short pathway. (No hiking map needed.)

Directions: From the intersection of US Hwys. 64 and 276 *South,* in downtown Brevard, *North Carolina,* drive south for 6 miles to the parking area on the west side of US 276.

Located on private property, but easily reached, Connestee Falls is one of the Brevard area's most popular destinations.

From the parking area, walk a winding path for 165' to the viewing area of this double waterfall. At your feet, Connestee Falls plunge 30' then run 40', plunging again, to commingle with the waters of Batson Creek Falls, which are seen 200' across the way.

Raven Cliff Falls, Greenville County, SC

Roads: Paved   A "10"
USGS Quadrangle: Table Rock, SC
Red blaze, 2.2 miles, moderate-difficult. To bridge and return, additional 4 miles.

This is one of my favorite hiking locales. I have just begun to scratch the surface of the vast Mountain Bridge Wilderness, which includes both Caesar's Head, and Jones Gap state parks. Here, the Appalachian Mountains rise abruptly out of South Carolina's foothills. Witness this dramatic change in the landscape from trailside overlooks, but especially when looking to the east from the Raven Cliff Fall's observation deck.

Of special note, is the cable and timber, suspension footbridge atop Raven Cliff Fall's upper tier. (This is accessed via a loop trail, described below.) Southern mountain scenery doesn't get any better than this. Plan to spend a day here.

Making my entry via trail #11, after intersecting the Foothills Trail (#13) I then made a loop of trails 13, 14, 12, and 11. To top it off, I then visited the Raven Cliff Fall's observation deck.

The well-constructed loop ranks among the toughest trails that I've hiked. Perhaps 1/4th of 1% of the park's visitors make this difficult hike. Descending Raven Cliff with 30 lbs on my back was no picnic. Crossing Matthews Creek on the cableway then ascending the opposing mountain was arduous, to say

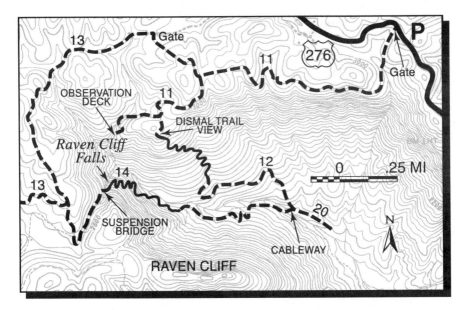

the least. If you plan to make the loop, hike it in a counterclockwise manner. I would much rather *descend* Raven Cliff's switchbacks than *ascend* them. Better yet, hike to the bridge via #13 and #14 and return the same way.

Listed after the fall's hike are the loop's landmarks and highlights.

Directions: From the intersection of US Hwys. 64 and 276 *South,* in downtown Brevard, *North Carolina,* drive south for 14.4 miles to the parking area, on the east side of US 276. The trail treads the gated service road on the *west* side of 276.

Alternate directions: If visiting Caesar's Head State Park, SC, drive north on 276 for 1.1 miles (from the visitor center) to the Raven Cliff parking area, which is on the right.

Enter the woods on the gated service road. This road carries the blue blaze of the Foothills Trail (#13) and the red blaze of the Raven Cliff Falls Trail (#11).

Descending moderately, in .2 of a mile arrive at a small outbuilding. Road gives way to trail after crossing the culvert and dam of a drained lake. Ascending while rounding the mountain, the trail soon levels out. Now following the mountainside, much like a contour line, at .7 of a mile tread a rocky stretch, then begin a gradual ascent. (In this vicinity, the trail, which has been treading an old, overgrown logging road, leaves that road to shortcut a hollow.) At .8 of a mile, atop bedrock, make a 90° bend right and meander through a laurel thicket. The trail soon bends left to descend stairs. With a right turn at their base, descend still further. After tracing a hollow, the trail bends right and turns steeply uphill, over a rocky and root-laced stretch. At 1.1 miles the trail rejoins the logging road and levels out. In approximately .1 of a mile make a hard right atop a ridge. Heading generally west, pass to the north side of a small knob, and at 1.4 miles arrive at the junction of the Foothills Trail. (The blue-blazed Foothills Trail turns off to the right, while the red-blazed Raven Cliff Falls Trail leads left. Signs denote this intersection. See highlights of the loop, below.)

Continuing on the fall's trail, at 1.6 miles arrive at a window-like opening where the South Carolina foothills can be seen. (Raven Cliff can be seen here, but not the falls.) Notice the foothills to mountains transition. At 1.75 miles, after having descended in an "S" fashion, over a rocky stretch of trail, pass the Dismal Trail, which intersects from the left. The fall's trail descends further and at 1.9 miles passes beneath a canopy of rhododendron. The trail is on the north side of the mountaintop here, and rounds its west side, enroute to the south slope. For the last 400 to 500', the trail winds while descending steeply. It terminates at the observation deck (2.2 miles) where the falls are viewed approximately 800' across the gorge.

The falls leap 30' then run 200' as cascades, before plunging a wind-swept 70' from an undercut cliff, whose rock is streaked and stained with a woodland varnish.

Highlights of the Loop:

- .35 of a mile: Iron gate.
- .35+ Intersect and tread old roadbed.
- 1.6 miles: Intersect and tread pink-blazed Naturaland Trust Trail #14 (Mountain Bridge Trail) on left.
- 1.95 miles: Small waterfall to right.
- 2 miles: Suspension bridge atop Raven Cliff Falls.
- 2.4 miles: Pass beneath 80-90' cliffs.
- 3 miles: Cross Matthews Creek on the cableway.
- 3.3 miles: Intersect and tread Dismal Trail #12.
- 4.55 miles: Dismal Trail View, Raven Cliff Falls, lower portion of falls visible 1200' across gorge.
- 4.7 miles: Intersect Raven Cliff Falls Trail #11.

Other Books by the Author

WATERFALL WALKS and DRIVES in GEORGIA, ALABAMA, and TENNESSEE

ISBN 0-9636070-2-2

A complete guide to the region's waterfalls. Day hikes only, leading to more than 125 waterfalls. One hundred fifty two pages of detailed driving and hiking directions, with more than 60 topographic hiking maps. Color photos and instructions on how to capture them on film for yourself.

Available at book and outdoor stores in the Southeast or, send check or money order for $9.95 to:

H.F. Publishing, Inc.
4552 E. Elmhurst Dr.
Suite "A"
Douglasville, GA. 30135

Please add $2.00 shipping and handling per address. Please allow 4 weeks for delivery. GA. residents add 5% sales tax.

NOTES